Rosa Prouincialis Dod.   *R. cum priore.*

The Gardens of
Queen Elizabeth

The
Queen Mother

A Personal Tour with
The Marchioness of Salisbury

With photographs by Derry Moore

Salem House Publishers
Topsfield, Massachusetts

First published in the United States by Salem House Publishers, 1988
462 Boston Street, Topsfield, MA 01983.

Text copyright © The Marchioness of Salisbury, 1988
Illustrations: the acknowledgements on p. 192 constitute an extension of the copyright page
All rights reserved. Without limiting the rights under copyright reserved
above, no part of this publication may be reproduced, stored
in or introduced into a retrieval system, or transmitted, in any form
or by any means (electronic, mechanical, photocopying,
recording or otherwise), without the prior written permission of both
the copyright owner and the above publisher of this book

Edited by Celia Van Oss
Designed by Yvonne Dedman

Typeset in Linotron Bembo
by Wyvern Typesetting Limited, Bristol
Printed by Olivotto, Vicenza, Italy

Library of Congress Cataloging-in-Publication Data
Salisbury, Marjorie Gascoyne-Cecil, 1922–
The gardens of Queen Elizabeth, the Queen Mother.
 1. Gardens—Great Britain—Pictorial works.
 2. Elizabeth, Queen, Consort of George VI, King of
  Great Britain, 1900– —Homes and haunts—
   Pictorial works. I. Title.
SB466.G7S35 1988 712'.6'0941   87–28790
   ISBN 0–88162–358–X

Frontispiece: The Queen Mother and the author in the garden of the Castle of Mey.
Endpapers: An engraving of the French *Rosa provincalis* of 1660 by Nicolas Robert. Queen Elizabeth loves the subtle beauty of the old-fashioned roses.

Contents

The Queen Mother's
Pleasure Gardens

There has been through the centuries a tradition of what we might call 'Queenly' gardening. Sovereigns and their consorts, or widows of sovereigns, who have loved their gardens and the flowers, trees and plants that have grown in them are not rare in recorded history. Some have been admirers only, others have been gardeners rather than plantsmen, and occasionally both skills have been combined. In our own times this tradition has been followed with enthusiasm and loving interest by Queen Elizabeth The Queen Mother, who has brought to her four gardens the individuality of her own special taste.

One of the earliest Queens of England to be a gardener was Philippa of Hainaut, wife of Edward III, who was noted for her herber, though perhaps she was more famous for having saved the lives of the Burghers of Calais from the wrath of her husband. This herber was made for her in the park at Odiham in 1332 – six oak trees, no less, were felled just to make boards for the paling and benches and there were five doors, so it must have been a fair size. She brought rosemary plants from Antwerp and grew, as we know from the records of Henry Daniel, a Dominican friar, many uncommon plants.

In the latter part of the fourteenth century Richard II's Queen, Anne, had a vineyard; 300 years later Anne of Denmark, married to James I, created a remarkable garden at Somerset House, her palace by the river Thames, with Isaac de Caus and Inigo Jones as her designers. Charles I's wife, Henrietta Maria, was named the 'Rose and Lily Queen' not only because of her French blood and marriage to the English king but also for her great love of gardening; she brought the great garden designer André Mollet over from France to work for her, and her gardens at Wimbledon and Oatlands, where John Tradescant was her gardener, were famous in their day.

Opposite: A charming statue of Charity is the focal point of one of the woodland rides at Royal Lodge. Her Majesty has always loved the original lead statue by John Cheere at St Paul's Waldenbury in Hertfordshire, and had it copied for her own garden.

Charles I with his French wife Henrietta Maria (known as the 'Rose and Lily Queen'), who was a passionate gardener.

At the end of the seventeenth century Mary, Queen to William III, sent gardeners to the Canary Islands, Virginia and other foreign parts to collect rare and exotic plants and seeds which she grew at Hampton Court Palace. She raised some of her botanical collection in the palace hothouses and laid out new gardens with the help and advice of George London (a pupil of Charles II's famous gardener, Rose).

George II's Queen, Caroline of Anspach, extended the gardens at Kensington Palace into Hyde Park and experimented with the picturesque in garden design, which was to be developed further by Queen Charlotte, the wife of George III, at Kew Palace.

Another royal lady who gardened enthusiastically was Princess Augusta, the wife of George II's eldest son. However, she never gardened as a Queen, for her husband died before his father. None the less, while living at Kew during her widowhood she was advised by Lord Bute, a skilled amateur botanist, and made, within a walled garden of nine acres, the first botanic garden of any size in England.

In our own century Queen Mary, wife of George V, also took a great interest in flowers and gardens. She loved to visit Kew when the bluebells were out, and during the Second World War, which she spent largely at Badminton House, the Duke and Duchess of Beaufort's home in Gloucestershire, she would spend many hours removing ivy from the trees in the grounds and woods round the house. She delighted in making visits to celebrated gardens, and there is a rose garden in Regent's Park, London, which is to this day known as 'Queen Mary's Rose Garden'.

The seeds of Queen Elizabeth The Queen Mother's own gardening style were sown in her early childhood, and nurtured and encouraged by the influences she encountered at home through her mother, Lady Strathmore, and her grandmother (who created a beautiful garden at the Villa Caponi, Florence), both keen gardeners. During her marriage to George VI, who had a considerable knowledge and love of plants and gardening, these were further developed, while Her Majesty was always close to her brother, Sir David Bowes Lyon, who was for many years President of the Royal Horticultural Society. His gardens at St Paul's Waldenbury in Hertfordshire were those of a fine plantsman, and were the scene of a large part of Queen Elizabeth's childhood. In later years Her Majesty would pay regular visits to her brother and his wife (also an outstanding gardener), admiring and enjoying the results of their gardening skills, and since her brother's death, those of his son, her nephew.

There are many different manifestations of Queen Elizabeth's interest in gardening, such as her treasured Chelsea 'Hans Sloane' botanical plates.

A love of gardening is often born in childhood, when the young are encouraged by their parents and their eyes are opened through hearing talk of gardens, flowers and plants. The first gift of packets of seeds and a little plot of ground to plan and plant at will can give the first taste of what may become a lifetime's pleasure. I think too that a talent for gardening, like other talents such as music and painting, can be inherited, and that, given her distinguished gardening family with their strong traditions, this may be true of Queen Elizabeth The Queen Mother.

Her Majesty is not only interested in her own gardens; she enjoys looking round the gardens of friends and relations and never fails to pay a visit to the Royal Horticultural Society's Chelsea Flower Show in May. Every year she visits Londoners' gardens as patron of the London Garden Society, and she is an active patron of numerous other gardening charities.

Above: Lady Elizabeth Bowes Lyon, aged two, with her sister Rose in the garden at St Paul's Waldenbury (August 1902).
Opposite: Queen Elizabeth The Queen Mother in 1909 at her Scottish home, Glamis Castle. Her Majesty acknowledges that her love of gardening was born in her childhood.

Royal Lodge was the first real home of the Duke and Duchess of York and, in the years before the Second World War, they worked hard to create an exceptional garden there. The sweeping lawns and secret woodland must have made it a perfect place for a young family to grow up in.

Of the four homes of Queen Elizabeth The Queen Mother, none can be separated from the charm of their setting; although they are each totally different in character and architecture and in the grounds and country that surround them, in their gardens at least they share a remarkable unity.

Royal Lodge, a delightful pink-washed Gothic house set in the middle of Windsor Park, has been the Queen Mother's home since 1931. Its superb woodland garden was created by the royal couple when they were Duke and Duchess of York, and today it retains many happy family memories for Her Majesty. Most of her weekends (when she is not in Scotland) are spent in the tranquillity of the Lodge, and it is of course within easy reach of her family when the Queen is at Windsor Castle. The garden is at its best in June, when the many rhododendrons and azaleas are in flower, and during this month (which is also the month of Ascot) the Queen Mother has a succession of small house parties for her friends.

The garden at Clarence House, where Her Majesty lives during the week, is a little more formal. Here she has her offices and provides hospitality for state visitors as well as personal ones. The walled garden is surprisingly large for London and is similar in atmosphere to nearby St James's Park, dominated as it is by magnificent plane trees. It is in use throughout the year, but is at its peak for Trooping the Colour at the beginning of June.

The Castle of Mey is special to Her Majesty because she found and chose it herself. The ancient, but light and welcoming castle is built of rosy granite and nestles in a hollow on the romantic Scottish coast, not far from John o'Groats. Within this awesome northern setting the Queen Mother has succeeded in making a magical cottage garden. During her visits in August and October, a mass of flowers grows among and alongside abundant fruit and vegetables, sheltered by high walls and thick tapestry hedges.

Finally, there is Birkhall, the Queen Mother's house on Royal Deeside which is but a good walk from Balmoral. The house is of simple white-painted stone with a lichen-covered slate roof, and has marvellous views over the bubbling brown waters of the river Muick to the moorlands beyond. Spring bulbs and

Left: George VI planted many varieties of rhododendron at Royal Lodge, and this *loderi* hybrid was named 'King George' in acknowledgement of his enthusiasm and expertise.
Right: Rosa rugosa 'Blanc Double de Coubert', one of the old-fashioned roses which Queen Elizabeth loves so well.

Her Majesty Queen Elizabeth The Queen Mother celebrating her eightieth birthday on 4 August 1980 in the gardens of Royal Lodge.

Two of Her Majesty's favourite flowers, pansies and azaleas, are depicted in this delightful painting in her collection by Henri Fantin-Latour.

blossom deck the garden when Her Majesty arrives in May for the salmon fishing on the Dee, and in August, when the whole family is on holiday at Balmoral, she likes to wander with her dogs along the river bank and up and down the slopes of her garden. Here steep beds and slopes are filled with the old–fashioned annuals, roses and herbaceous plants that Her Majesty loves so much.

Despite their distinctiveness, the gardens share a harmony of character and feeling which is sensed most strongly as you visit each one. This of course must be largely created by the style of gardening and the choice of plants dictated by the Queen Mother's taste – her likes and dislikes – but, as we walked around them, I felt there was more than this. There was in each of the gardens a homeliness, an easy informality, a continuity with the past which gave a feeling of timelessness, the human and the natural seeming to be combined in felicitous union.

Here are four gardens that are loved and cherished. Intensely personal, they blossom under a hand and eye that sees and knows, and whose gardeners are united in their dedication to achieving perfection.

Royal Lodge

WINDSOR

oyal Lodge is one of several lodges and houses set in the Great Park at Windsor which were the handiwork of successive sovereigns and the Rangers who served them. The Park has been the preserve of royalty for many hundreds of years; part of the King's woodland was enclosed as early as 1086. Much of its beauty then can be imagined now, as we look at the bracken and the hawthorn, the elder, the herds of deer and the great oaks with their spreading branches and huge trunks – some looking like fossils in their ancient greyness, standing stag-headed and stalwart although centuries have passed. The scene cannot be very different from the one viewed in the days when the park was largely primeval forest.

In medieval times Windsor Great Park was divided into several different smaller parks, encompassing varying acreages of land. In Henry III's time the Constable of the Castle was ordered to sell wood in Windsor Park and to enclose it out of the proceeds of the sale, and by Edward III's reign we hear of the enclosed new park at Windsor called Wythemere. Under Edward IV, 200 acres adjoining the town of New Windsor were enclosed; this was a large addition to, or perhaps the origin of, what is now the Home Park. Later Lord Burleigh, Elizabeth I's chief minister, anxious that the Forest of Dean (the chief source of timber for the country's fighting ships) might be threatened by the Spaniards, planted thirteen acres of oaks in part of the area of Windsor Park called Cranbourne Park. At this time there were many herds of fallow and red deer roaming the park, and the forest provided sport and a plentiful supply of

Opposite: The Gothic front of the Lodge. Mobile trellis on the terrace provides shelter for Queen Elizabeth, who likes to be out in her garden throughout the seasons.

Paul Sandby's watercolour of *c.* 1800, *View in the Gardens of the Deputy Ranger's House*, shows the Royal Lodge gardens to have been very much part of the park before the house was lived in by a member of the Royal Family.

food – but venison was not the only food to be found there, for fish such as bream and pike were plentiful in the ponds and rivers, while heron, wild cattle and rabbits abounded. The deer remained until 1942, being dispersed in that year, but thirty-five years later they were re-established in a new deer park. In 1631 visitors to the park could take part in 'the pleasant pastime arising out of the forest, chace, and fourteen parks that waite upon it', and it is still the scene for such pastimes today – riding, shooting, driving and fishing – not to mention farming, forestry and deer-breeding.

Opposite: Ancient oaks and Spanish chestnuts provide a stately approach to Royal Lodge. They are particularly lovely in autumn, when the grass is still a verdant sward and the bases of the trees are sprinkled with bright coppery leaves.

Medieval parks, unlike the landscaped parks of the eighteenth century, were divorced from houses, and it was not until William, Duke of Cumberland, became Park Ranger for King George II that the woodland rides and glades, the ponds and lakes, appeared linked with houses in the park – such as Cumberland Lodge and the house that was to become Royal Lodge and ultimately one of the homes of Queen Elizabeth The Queen Mother.

Of the four houses and their gardens lived in by the Queen Mother, Royal Lodge may well be the one most truly home to her. For it was to this house with its rose-washed walls, with no pretensions of stately grandeur or noble architecture, but with the charm of being a real home, that the late King George VI and Queen Elizabeth came in 1931 when Duke and Duchess of York, and it was largely here that they brought up their two daughters, the future Queen Elizabeth and their second child, Princess Margaret Rose. The house, loaned to their Royal Highnesses by George V, had seen many changes both to its structure and in the people who inhabited it, for its history goes back to the early years of the eighteenth century when it was a simple red brick house built as houses typically were in the reign of Queen Anne. It was called Lower Lodge then, as it was not occupied by a member of the Royal Family but by the Deputy Ranger of the Great Park, one Thomas Sandby. The Ranger of the Great Park lived in the Great Lodge (soon to become known as Cumberland Lodge), and from 1764 the Ranger was George, Duke of Cumberland. The Lower Lodge was a habitation of lesser importance, but was occupied until the early years of the nineteenth century by those variously involved in the farming and development of the Great Park.

The Lower Lodge was not much longer to remain a simple Queen Anne house. In 1811 George III was on the throne, but his increasing madness made it necessary for his son to act as Prince Regent and, in order to carry out his duties, the Prince had to find somewhere to live that was near to both London and Windsor. His eye fell on Cumberland Lodge, then unoccupied, and while this was being adapted to his needs he moved into the Lower Lodge. We well know of the extravagance of the Prince Regent, his passion for building, his grand 'folly' in Brighton, and the British public's increasing impatience with and hostility to the seemingly endless expenditure on the houses he occupied. The Lower Lodge was to be no exception; indeed, it was to be one of the most extravagant of all the Prince's architectural fancies and it was not long before its name was changed to the Royal Lodge. However, much was to happen to it before it became generally known by that name, it having quickly acquired among the public the titles of 'King's Cottage' and 'Thatched Palace', not without a certain tone of mockery and sarcasm.

For this 'cottage', in the hands of the Prince's architect of the woods and forests, John Nash (who had been responsible for some of the great rooms at

An engraving after a drawing by Delamotte, 1824, showing Royal Lodge as a *cottage orné*,
transformed by Nash for the Prince Regent at the end of the eighteenth century.

Carlton House and other buildings for George IV when he was Prince Regent),
soon developed into something quite different. Building was to its new owner a
passion close to mania, but to compensate for his many faults and follies the
Regent was a true connoisseur of the arts and a most generous patron. Weighing
not much under 17 stone at the age of forty-eight, he was none the less a graceful
man, who still bore traces of the handsome looks of his youth, coupled with
considerable urbanity and charm.

He asked Nash, who was an architect of exceptional talent, to produce
designs that were to turn a simple house into a romantic retreat among the
glades and groves of Windsor Park. At first Nash's plans seemed modest, the
initial estimate for the works being under £3,000, but this expenditure was
rapidly and extravagantly exceeded as the alterations became more elaborate
and the extensions to the house spread. The final bill he presented in 1814 was
for £52,000. The entrance front was given gables and a Gothic door, tiles were
removed and replaced by thatch, sash windows became mullioned ones and
coloured plaster covered the russet brick walls. A large conservatory paned in

glass with 'cast iron trellissed pilasters' and a 'trellissed temple in the middle' reposed at the western end of the south front, and from this extended a broad veranda roofed in thatch and upheld by pillars in the rustic mode, wrapped in climbing plants of ivy and honeysuckle. The unpretentious house had become an elaborate and fashionable *cottage orné*, but a cottage it could hardly with truth be called, and even Nash tried to disguise the final size of his design by planting groves of trees here and there to confuse and deceive the eye. However, the tall and elegant chimneys which he had built in considerable numbers could not be hidden, and they proclaimed to all who viewed it the extent of the building. By the end of 1814 Nash had completed the initial developments, but renovations, additions and alterations continued under his direction, and later under that of the architect Jeffry Wyattville, until the death of George IV. The last development, the addition of a new dining-room (the only room to survive to the present day) was not finished by the time he died.

Costly and extravagant as the transformation of the house was, the results must have been delightful, and when the Prince Regent loaned it to his sister, Princess Elizabeth, for her honeymoon with the Hereditary Prince of the Hesse-Homburg, it would seem there could be no more appealing setting for romance. However, the bridegroom rather spoils the picture our fancy might have conjured, as it appears that he was a supremely unromantic figure – hugely fat, no longer young and smelling of garlic and tobacco – and spent much of the honeymoon smoking in the conservatory.

In 1820 poor mad old George III, the Prince Regent's father, died, but during the nine years of the Regency the feeling in the country against the future George IV had steadily grown and he could hardly appear even briefly in public without being insulted. As King, he found life in the capital more and more insupportable and retreated increasingly to the seclusion of Royal Lodge, where he would enjoy the peace and tranquillity of the lawns and glades surrounding his house in the Great Park. Here he would drive himself out in a phaeton down the long and broad rides in the plantations he had created to adorn the land about his 'cottage'. His disappearance from public view only further stimulated the people's feelings against him, and they accused him of cowardice because he would not show himself to them. This did not, however, prevent the King from continuing his pleasurable building operations, or from enjoying his rustic retirement.

In June 1830 George IV died and was succeeded by his brother William, who as Duke of Clarence had lived at what is now the London home of Queen Elizabeth The Queen Mother – Clarence House. He was a very different character who was popular with the mob, showing them an amiable familiarity and being blunt and genial with all. He had a simple unaffected manner and disapproved of the excesses of his late brother, cutting down on the numbers of

George IV Taking His Favourite Exercise near the Sandpit Gate, Windsor Park (engraving by Melville, 1830). Even when the Prince Regent became king he spent a large amount of time relaxing in his Windsor retreat.

staff and drastically pruning the luxurious establishments set up by the last King. One of his economies was to reduce the size of Royal Lodge; in fact he pulled the largest part of it down, leaving Wyattville's last addition, a large saloon facing west which is now the drawing-room of the present house. The conservatory and adjacent chapel were to be added to the lawn and garden of Cumberland Lodge, and some of the materials from the demolished Lodge were used in the construction of a small cottage designed and built by Wyattville in 1831 for Queen Adelaide. The Chancellor of the Exchequer was informed by the Deputy Ranger in 1830 that:

> . . . the additions that His late Majesty made at this place were always rapidly constructed, for temporary convenience; the building had no vaulted foundation and was consequently in winter hardly habitable for its dampness; the roof, only one storey in height, was so extended and varied as to require constant and increasing expense; the building had no lodgements for the necessary attendants on a royal establishment, and was in every way unfit for such a purpose. When His present Majesty made a personal survey of this building, he could not but observe these defects, and having determined to reside in His Palace at Windsor, he no longer wished to impose on the public the burden of maintaining Royal Lodge, at an

expense of at least five thousand pounds per annum. With this view His Majesty ordered the principal part of the building and paled enclosure to be taken down, the materials of the building to go in aid of the building of Windsor Castle; the paling extending around the premises nearly two miles, and applied in repair of the outward fences of the Park . . .

The saloon, which was the only part of Royal Lodge left standing, became part of a far more modest house which was constructed in the later half of the nineteenth century. It was not until 1874 that the building was once more regularly occupied, when various court officials lived there; a Major Fetherstonhaugh, manager of King George V's racing stables, was the last occupant before the King lent it to the Duke and Duchess of York. Certainly no horticultural interest had been shown in the surroundings of Royal Lodge since the days of George IV. William IV's nearest interest was an occasional visit to Virginia Water, where he and his entourage would embark on the lake in a barge and fish while a band played to the party from another boat, it being said that his hunger for the sea was assuaged partly by being able to navigate on these waters, and partly by the attentions he paid to his farm and garden. There is no evidence, however, that he carried out any cultivation or planting of the latter or was particularly interested in horticulture.

Queen Elizabeth in the Savill Garden, Windsor, in the summer of 1964, accompanied by Sir Eric Savill (right) and Charles de Noailles. Sir Eric created this garden at the same time that the Duke and Duchess of York were making their gardens at Royal Lodge; their mutual support is evident in many of the two gardens' plantings.

In the year 1931 a great change was to come over Royal Lodge, its garden and the woodlands around it, for that was the year, as we have seen, when it became the home of the Duke and Duchess of York. It was here at Royal Lodge that Queen Elizabeth's love of gardening, for the first time in her adult life, was able to take a practical form. This love had been born during her childhood, for her mother, Lady Strathmore, as Queen Elizabeth happily tells, was a great gardener. In the garden at Glamis in Scotland she has found the inspiration for much of her planting, for example her choice of flowers and plants grown in the gardens of earlier times – such as the old-fashioned roses and sweet peas, lilies and pansies.

The King and Queen's arrival at Royal Lodge, and their interest in the garden, came at a time when the Savill Garden was being created. Eric Savill was Deputy Ranger of Windsor Great Park, and his personal interest led to a request for a small budget for gardening. In 1932 a first small planting was established. This was a quarter-acre bog garden, visited in its early days by King George V and Queen Mary, who are supposed to have said, 'It's very nice Mr Savill, but isn't it very small?' This remark was to lead to the considerable expansion of the garden, not without much encouragement from King George VI and Queen Elizabeth, who were both developing the woodland and other parts of the gardens at Royal Lodge, and planting many of the same things Sir Eric was introducing to the gardens he was creating.

The layout and planting of the gardens at Royal Lodge are little changed from those you would have seen had you visited them in the 1930s, and Queen Elizabeth most understandably likes to keep them as unaltered as possible. She and the King planned and created the garden together, their special love and interest being the woodland garden. Here the King could indulge his affection for and very considerable knowledge of rhododendrons, azaleas and ornamental flowering trees, and the Queen her enthusiasm for the beautifully sculptured and fragrant flowers of magnolias and the charms of the woodland lilies.

Royal Lodge is in the south-east corner of Windsor Great Park and is surrounded by about thirty acres of grounds and garden. You approach it from the north through two neo-classical lodges, their walls washed in the same rosy pink as the main house, their windows and doors framed and pedimented in creamy stone. The drive curves past a small Victorian Gothic church which in summer is embowered in roses, trained on its walls and along the iron railings surrounding it. An immense wisteria clambers up to the belfry, and within the enclosure there is Victorian carpet bedding of French marigolds, geraniums and lobelia. A gentle bend to the right and you find yourself in a gravelled forecourt, framed on all sides by sturdy buttressed walls of dark green clipped yew, and facing you is the rather austere east front of the house with its simple porch.

25

Like all the houses of Queen Elizabeth The Queen Mother, Royal Lodge has a friendly look and you feel at once an atmosphere that appeals to the senses. A hen pheasant crosses the forecourt, unhurrying, and a spotted woodpecker flies from a bird table suspended from the branches of a Japanese cherry tree which grows to the right of the front door; you are reminded that birds are one of the living things that go with flowers and trees to form, in combination with architecture and sculpture, the medium for the creation of an ideal garden.

Rising behind the yew hedge to the left of the house, some of their branches casting a lush shade, are fine trees forming a rich tapestry of greens and varied shapes. A tall dark conifer is there, two acers, *A. palmatum* and *A. platanoides*, a

A winter view of Royal Lodge and its gardens from the air.

Left: Rosa filipes 'Kiftsgate' scrambles high into one of the trees of the entrance court.
Right: The fascinatingly formed flowers of the tulip tree (*Liriodendron tulipifera*).

copper beech, golden privet and variegated ivy and holly which lighten with touches of gold the sombre backcloth. In late June *Rosa filipes* 'Kiftsgate', scrambling high into one of the trees, scents the air, while earlier in the month some gentle colour is provided by lilac, deutzia, and an old pink hybrid rhododendron. But the finest and most interesting tree in this plantation is the tulip tree (*Liriodendron tulipifera*), a magnificent specimen which must be over 60 feet high and 40 feet across. Introduced from North America by John Tradescant, it was known to have been grown by Bishop Compton in his palace garden at Fulham in 1688, and was almost certainly growing elsewhere much earlier than this. Here at Royal Lodge it flowers abundantly in July, with tulip-shaped blossoms of a green-white with a large orange blotch at their base. Another delightful shrub which I noticed planted in the gravel against the yew hedge on this side of the entrance court is *Rosa glauca*. A sheaf of strong thorn-covered stems shoots upwards, bursting into a cloudy mass of purplish-grey; the young stems of the rose are plum-red, and the clustered single flowers are a clear pink, later to be transformed into deep red hips.

Digging for Victory – the Royal Princesses join in the war effort in 1940. Much of the Royal Lodge gardens was ploughed up to grow vegetables.

Either side of the entrance porch, under the walls of the Lodge, are narrow borders, planted in late spring with mixed wallflowers, polyanthus, and the lily-flowered tulip 'Maytime', with its elegantly curving petals giving it an eastern look. Flowering crab trees (*Malus floribunda*) and may (*Crataegus oxycantha*) as well as the 'Kanzan' cherry (*Prunus serrulata purpurascens*) enliven the early summer scene. Later in the year the agapanthus ('Headbourne Worthy' hybrids) and day lilies (hemerocallis) are in gay flower on both sides of the yew hedges at the entrance, and the borders under the house are filled with mixed zonal pelargoniums. 'Sally Jones', 'Alice Greenfield', 'Tranquil', 'Wheel of Life', 'Jimmy Greaves' and 'Gentleman Jim Horton' are all here, with leaves as vivid in their way as the single-petalled flowers – brilliant gold, yellow and the deepest green, while a young rosemary bush (*Rosmarinus officinalis*), planted by a pillar of the porch, will soon scent the passage of those going in and out of the house.

Leaving the entrance court and turning right through an iron wicket gate in the yew hedge, you find yourself in a partial enclosure fringed by small ornamental trees, where shrubs, planted in borders, surround formal beds of hybrid musk roses; in the centre is a lead statue of Orpheus with his lyre, which used to be at Clarence House. It was in this enclosure that the two Princesses used to have their gardens, with their own sets of tools, a little tool house, a seat and a barrow, where they would grow rock plants, aubrieta and the other simple cottage garden flowers that children love. Though much changed, there are still plants that were here in those days such as a graceful *Acer japonicum* 'Vitifolium' and a *Salix matsudana* 'Tortuosa' (grown from a cutting taken by Queen Elizabeth herself – it is called the dragon's claw willow and is a most interesting plant which came from Northern China in the 1920s and has strange, contorted twigs and branches). There is a *Laburnum × watereri* 'Vossii' too, planted near several philadelphus varieties with their waxy white flowers, some of them so highly scented that, as Gerard wrote more than 300 years ago: '. . . they trouble and molest the head in a very strange manner . . . I gathered the flowers and laid them in my chamber window, which smelled more strongly after they had lain together for a few hours, but with such a pontick and unaquainted savor that they awakened me from sleepe, so that I could not rest till I had cast them out of my chamber.'

Queen Elizabeth has other scented shrubs of great beauty in this little garden: there is *Magnolia stellata*, whose bark is fragrant as well as its flowers, and not far from its small neat form grows a Japanese apricot, *Prunus mume*. This ravishingly pretty small blossom tree or bush with sweet-smelling flowers has been cultivated in China for the pleasure of its appearance for over 1,500 years, and in Japan for almost as long. It arrived in this country in 1841 and, although it does like a sheltered place, it is not hard to grow. Such is its loveliness that I cannot

Left: Viburnum × burkwoodii, which bears its sweetly scented flowers in rich clusters during April and May.
Right: Rosa glauca is among the best of the rose family for autumn display and is allowed to grow freely at Royal Lodge.

imagine why it is not planted more. In another corner is a large bush of *Viburnum × burkwoodii*, pink-budded white flowers covering it from top to bottom in fragrant beauty through April and May. *Mahonia japonica* is growing here too, its long racemes of lemon-yellow flowers smelling strongly of lily-of-the-valley. Pick a whole stem carrying its cluster of pendulous racemes, split it well (for it is stiff and woody), removing the prickly leaves, and put it in a vase in your room – it is often in flower before Christmas – and you will be ravished by the scent.

In spring a *Malus floribunda* near the house is a froth of palest pink blossom with cherry-coloured buds, and the shrubs are underplanted with a bright mixture of polyanthus, wallflowers and the elegant small narcissus 'March Sunshine'. But it is the sense of smell that is appealed to most strongly in this part of the garden, and we are reminded of Queen Elizabeth's special love of scented flowers and plants as we note the number Her Majesty has herself planted here.

To leave the forecourt from the other side and reach the southern and western parts of the garden, which are screened by a wall, we pass through a wooden gate, its upper half pierced by lattice work in the Chinese manner. We find ourselves standing on the south terrace, broad and flagged, which surrounds the house; it is edged by a low wall which on its far side drops a considerable height to the sweeping lawns below. From here we look left on to a formal rose garden, enclosed on three sides by high yew and beech hedges. Geoffrey Jellicoe and Russell Page were mainly responsible for the design of this garden and of the terraces which skilfully link the architecture with its setting, but the rose garden has recently been completely re-planted, the old soil being renewed with quantities of superb loam and barrowfuls of well-rotted farmyard manure. New rose plants have been introduced, gifts from the Prince of Wales and the Duke of Grafton to Her Majesty, and within another year or two it should once more be a fine sight. Here nature is disciplined: the roses are enclosed in an orderly arrangement, the beds are divided by York stone flagged paths and walled in by the clipped russet or spring green of the beech and the darkness of the yew, but within the formality the roses will grow free, for Queen Elizabeth does not like them to be pruned severely. Besides, the majority are 'old-fashioned roses', the Centifolias, Albas, Portlands, Damasks, Gallicas and Bourbons, which need the lightest of touches with the knife. With a subtle beauty and grace of colour, shape and scent, these are the roses that Her Majesty loves so well, their flowers in velvety purples, crimsons and burgundies, ashy lavenders and pink, sometimes striped and slashed with carmine and rose on white, sometimes creamy white with jade-green button eyes and quartered flowers – their charm is captivating. Planted among them are some more modern roses; I saw 'Swany', grown here as a standard and covered with snow-white very double cupped flowers, 'The Fairy' with a profusion of pale pink flowers, and the Japanese rose 'Nozomi' with single pearly-pink flowers. There are five or six Rugosa roses too, their leaves rough-textured and wrinkled, their flowers heavily scented, huge hips boldly studding the bushes in autumn with scarlet and deepest flame. Modern shrub roses are represented by 'Angelina' with its very fragrant pink flowers; the hybrid musks by 'Ballerina', 'Prosperity', that great beauty with creamy, sunset-touched buds and flowers, 'Penelope', and the newest of the hybrid musks, 'Sadlers Wells'; while there is a bush of a species rose, *R. woodsii fendlerii*, with single pink flowers and greyish twiggy growth that will be covered in the autumn with deep scarlet hips. Several plants grow against the terrace wall in the rose garden: *R. sinica* 'Anemonoides' with its single pink flowers (a special favourite of Queen Elizabeth's), *Viburnum × burkwoodii*, and an old chaenomeles.

Altogether it is a very catholic collection of roses, with nearly every 'family' represented; the garden will surely be a delight to Queen Elizabeth as it

This beautiful old pink peony is one of the stars of the new herbaceous border.

develops, for the burgeoning and billowing of the roses within the straight and strict lines of the beds successfully combines elements of the formal and informal, and in thus uniting art and nature creates a delightful harmony.

From the terrace at this point we can survey the border which, like the rose garden, has recently been completely re-planted and built up with new soil. It is backed by the yew hedge which is one of the 'walls' of the rose garden and runs from below the terrace towards the woodland garden – it has herbaceous plants and a few roses, one a very pretty pink called 'St Helena'. There are phloxes, 'White Admiral', 'Tenor', 'Balmoral' and 'Windsor' among them; lupins – the beautiful creamy-white 'Noble Maiden', and 'My Castle'; delphinium 'Blue Bees' and herbaceous peonies, including the delicious, very old 'Duchesse de Nemours', seldom seen but one of the very best, with its fat creamy-white

Opposite above: Hybrid musks 'Prosperity' (*left*) and 'Ballerina' (*right*) are among the wide variety of roses given to Her Majesty by the Duke of Grafton for her new rose garden.
Opposite below: Clear pink and very fragrant, like many of the Queen Mother's favourite flowers, the floribunda rose 'Elizabeth of Glamis' is worthy of Her Majesty's name.

scented flowers crammed with petals. *Anchusa italica* 'Little John', erigerons, pyrethrums and several other unusual varieties of herbaceous plants catch my eye.

From where we have been standing on the southern part of the terrace looking on to the rose garden and the border, we turn and look back at the house and along the length of the terrace, to admire a wisteria, *sinensis alba*, surrounding the gate we ca...ne in by, its racemes of flowers showing snowy white against the rose-washed wall. *Wisteria sinensis* was first grown in this country in 1816, having been brought from China where it grew in the Canton garden of a Chinese merchant. A few years later, in 1824, John Parks brought back another native of China, the Banksian rose, and its cultivar 'Lutea' now grows at Royal Lodge on the wall near the white wisteria. This particular plant has not yet flowered, but when mature it will, and the month of May will see its small-leaved, light green shiny foliage covered in hanging sprays of faintly scented double yellow flowers. Another older plant of this same rose grows below the terrace wall facing the rose garden, and this one flowers abundantly.

But now a stronger smell assails our nostrils, that of the lavender, *Lavandula* 'Hidcote', which edges a rectangular bed and narrow border under the terrace wall. Both of these are planted with the rose 'Elizabeth of Glamis', a pink floribunda named of course after Her Majesty and underplanted in the spring

Queen Elizabeth at Royal Lodge in 1970. The planting of forget-me-nots and tulips is the same in another corner of the terrace today.

with forget-me-nots and 'Clara Butt' tulips. This sturdy Darwin tulip has neat, small, pure pink flowers of perfect form and is as loved now as when it was first introduced in the years before the last war. In the summer the beds are planted with the zonal pelargonium 'King of Denmark', its flowers the same pink as the tulips and matching the roses perfectly. Much of the lavender has lately had to be replaced as it had become too old and woody, but with its swift growth it will soon regain its former splendour.

The Royal Lodge gardens are under the expert supervision of Mr John Bond, who succeeded Sir Eric Savill as director of the Savill and Valley Gardens, but a permanent head gardener, Mr Bennett, has recently been appointed to Royal Lodge and he has three men working for him all the year round. Mr Bond has had the job of directing the re-planting of the rose garden, as well as the thinning of the overgrowth in the woodland garden. This has been a delicate task, as he has had to be very sure that he does not change the essential character of the garden that Queen Elizabeth so much loves. Her Majesty wishes to keep it as nearly as possible as she remembers it to have been when created by herself and the King. At the same time Mr Bond has had to renew and re-plant certain things that have grown too old, too woody and past their best.

On the wall of the house, covered in buds and looking very happy, is a *Fremontodendron* 'Californian Glory' which was presented to the Queen Mother

The distinctive mixture of 'Clara Butt' tulips and forget-me-nots on the terrace.

Above: Trees have been carefully planted to give an open outlook from the terrace as well as almost total privacy.

Below: In June the heady fragrance of *Rhododendron luteum* hits you as you round the corner of the terrace. Every shade of yellow, from palest lemon to burnt cinnamon, is to be seen in large island beds in the lawn and down a woodland ride.

by the famous nurseryman and plantsman, Harold Hillier. It is tall and evergreen, with large yellow flowers whose papery 'petals' are really calyxes. Coming from the west coast of the United States, it loves the sun, and is very happily placed here on the south-facing wall of the single-storeyed octagonal portion of Royal Lodge. At the feet of the fremontodendron is a clump of *Iris stylosa* (*synguicularis*), that native of Algeria which only flowers really well if thoroughly starved in the poorest of dry soils, its scented violet-blue flowers appearing in the depth of winter to cheer our hearts with thoughts of spring.

Below the terrace at this point the ground has been cut away and levelled, forming a sheltered place to sit. With its back to the retaining wall is a bronze of a child with arms outstretched, and a white-painted seat and chairs with Chinese Chippendale backs (in the manner of the terrace door we came through) are posed against the wall. The ground is paved with York stone, and two blocks of clipped yew jut out from the wall on either side of the seats to protect the retreat from the wind. Raised beds each side of the yew, their earth retained by pink-washed walls matching those of the terrace, are bedded out in spring and summer, and planted with *Nerine bowdenii* for autumn flowering.

The terrace continues round the west-facing two-storeyed part of the house; on the ground floor five large perpendicular Gothic windows light the drawing-room. White-painted tubs, planted with box clipped into conical shapes, are spaced along the top of the terrace wall, and large Chinese porcelain 'jar seats' stand by the windows, some blue and white and some a rainbow mixture of colours. They complement the exotic atmosphere created by the ogee windows, each capped with a crown carrying the initials of sovereigns from William IV to (above a window around the corner) George VI. Trelliswork terminates the terrace on the north-west, screening a planting of clipped beech and forming another sheltered sitting place for Her Majesty; this area can be made even more protected by glass screens that can be pulled out and arranged according to the direction of the wind. In this corner, two painted lions holding shields with gilded cyphers, 'GR III' and 'GR VI', sit high on narrow columns of trelliswork. The paving stones of the sitting area, the lines of which form a circle, are echoed by the curved seat and a circular terracotta-coloured marble table, supported by more lions, while steps curve down from the terrace to the lawns below.

When we walked around the corner of the terrace during my May visit to Royal Lodge, past the white-painted, scrolled urns, we were met by an extraordinarily strong fragrance wafting up from the garden beneath us. This I discovered came from two island beds of *Rhododendron luteum* (a deciduous rhododendron with a mass of yellow flowers) which are set in the undulating lawns below the terrace. The lie of the land, which slopes away to fields, hedgerows and woods, forms a charming vista – the fields in the spring green with young corn and in July yellowing ready for harvest. The transition from the formal treatment of the layout around the house to the informality of the sweeping and descending lawns, which meld in the most natural way into the wilderness of the woodland garden, is very skilful. So gradual is it that the eye senses no disharmony – indeed, the manner of one passes most easily into that of the other. This is a garden to be moved through, not just to be admired from above and afar, and it is with eager steps that we descend the curved stairs to the mossy lawns, thick in the month of August with the tiny wild yellow tormentil, but in May a vivid green.

The rabbits are very bold and a real pest in the garden (necessitating low wire barriers in some parts), and we disturbed one grazing on the lawn as we walked towards the woodland, inhaling the delectable scent of the yellow azaleas as we passed. Near to them is a fine stand of *Acer palmatum* and *A. palmatum* 'Dissectum', and to the left and right are a group of ancient oaks and two great cedars of Lebanon, striking in their quiet dignity. They and the circle of woodland, with its noble forest trees and close ornamental underplanting, make the garden at Royal Lodge a very private and secluded one. As we enter the woodland, past a bed filled with *Paeonia suffruticosa*, we can see the skilful planting in greater detail: on our right there is a *Magnolia grandiflora* hybrid of a particularly good variety called 'Maryland' (*virginiana* × *grandiflora*). Queen Elizabeth has special affection for the graceful, often fragrant flowers of these

Above: There are two specimens of *Magnolia grandiflora*, with its elaborate arrangement of sepals, stamens and pistils, at Royal Lodge. Queen Elizabeth has special affection for the graceful, fragrant flowers of the magnolia, and she has many different varieties in her gardens.
Opposite: A group of venerable Lebanon cedars dominates the lawn. These must date from the Prince Regent's changes to the Lodge.

Queen Elizabeth loves the wildness of the woodland garden at Royal Lodge and likes the plants to grow as naturally as possible. It is often difficult to tell where the garden ends and the ancient park of Windsor begins.

trees, some of which grow to the height and width of forest trees, others to a more modest size, but all with white, cream, pink or deep rose flowers pointing goblet-like to the sky or hanging suspended so that you may look up into them and see the elaborate arrangement of sepals, stamens and pistils. Her Majesty has planted many magnolias both here and in her London garden, and at Royal Lodge another venerable specimen grows on the terrace, its dark leaves contrasting well with the pink walls of the house.

In late spring not a leaf can be seen on the rhododendrons which stretch down either side of a broad green glade in the woodland garden; they are thick with flowers in yellows of every hue, from lemon shading through to burnt cinnamon. Gardeners in Japan treat azaleas as they occur in nature, and here at

The planting of this rich purple, spreading copper beech in front of the davidia and a group of tall conifers is typical of the inspired composition of so much planting at Royal Lodge.

Royal Lodge they are planted in the same way; however, over the years since they were planted by George VI and Queen Elizabeth, they have grown and spread and have had to be drastically trimmed and thinned under the direction of Mr Bond. Now they once more both arrest and enchant the eye, glowing like candle flames of light in the shaded woods.

The view at the end of this broad ride is closed by a bronze statue of Charity, which depicts a woman with her children and is a copy of one at St Paul's Waldenbury, Hertfordshire (*see page 6*). One of the Queen Mother's childhood homes, this was later the home of her brother, Sir David Bowes Lyon, whose expert knowledge of gardening and uncommon skills as a plantsman, Her Majesty acknowledges, greatly encouraged her love and interest in gardens and

plants. Beyond the statue rise the tall silver trunks of birch, a favourite tree of Queen Elizabeth, who has other fine specimens at Birkhall; beneath the canopy of trees first snowdrops and later bluebells and narcissi carpet the ground.

One of the most magnificent sights in the woodland garden in May are two *Davidia involucrata* trees, one of which is the biggest in the country. The davidia is perhaps the most beautiful of all the trees of the north temperate flora, and is much loved by Queen Elizabeth, who tells of her admiration for it, 'the marvellous aromatic smell it has at dusk', and of how the original tree planted at Royal Lodge produced a child which has grown and flourished to become almost as tall as its parent. The davidia was discovered near Hupin in China in 1869 by Abbé David, a teacher missionary and enthusiastic naturalist who was sent to China by the French government and who is chiefly remembered for this tree and the deer named after him. What astonishment and delight the Abbé must have felt as he gazed for the first time at this tree with flowers – or what must have seemed to him to be flowers – hovering among its leaves, gleaming white and elegant! Ernest Wilson, a later plant collector who took seeds with him back to England, described them as 'resembling huge butterflies when disturbed by the slightest breeze'. The flowers are in fact three bracts which hang like a canopy over the flower-heads and look like white handkerchiefs, giving the davidia its other name, the 'handkerchief tree'.

Opposite: Bluebells carpet the woodland in spring. The glades are romantic all the year round, and it is easy to understand why Queen Elizabeth finds so many memories here.
Below: The large hanging bracts of the davidia have given this beautiful and unusual tree the nickname of the 'handkerchief tree'.

Of the many plants discovered by Abbé David (he is said to have walked thirty miles a day in search of rare specimens), a large number are found in the plantings of the woodland garden at Royal Lodge. The mixture of musk roses, gentians, rhododendrons, primulas, clematis and buddleia which the Abbé found growing naturally in the wild is reproduced here, and this may well be one of the secrets of its harmony and charm. The selection shows the skilled plantsmanship and taste of George VI and his Queen, who introduced them in the 1930s when they were creating the garden. It makes it a place of especially treasured memories for the Queen Mother, who feels that the woodland garden is the true garden of Royal Lodge and that it is at its most glorious in the spring when the rhododendron glades are in full flower and the trees still freshly verdant.

Many of the rhododendrons are plants of _R. loderi_, crossed in 1901 and introduced between 1935 and 1938 when numerous hybrids were developed; one (from _fortunei_ × _griffithianum_) is called 'King George' as a tribute to His late Majesty. This hybrid group, which has fragrant white flowers and buds of apple blossom pink, is named after Sir Edmund Loder who had many plants in his famous gardens at Leonardslee in Sussex. The plants at Royal Lodge were badly damaged by heavy falls of snow in 1981, but new young rhododendron species are here too, as well as some good hybrids given to Queen Elizabeth by Mr Edmond de Rothschild.

Though the wood is furnished with many ancient trees, some towering and dark like the great redwood (_Sequoia sempervirens_) which rises beyond the statue, and the cedar of Lebanon, among them is a glorious weeping beech and the impression that the woodlands give is one of lightness and gaiety. The mosses in varying greens are close and bright. Ferns spring from bank and tussock, and the ground you tread is soft and strewn with wild flowers, while in the thin grass in the month of August, tall Turk's-cap lilies grow. The amber bark of the redwood glows in the shade and clustered silver birch shoot their parchment-coloured trunks up to the canopy of leaves above, darkening and glimmering under a filtered sun. The spotted leaves of _Pulmonaria officinale_ push through the ferns, white marked (the old tales tell us) by drops of Our Lady's milk, while in early spring, shadows are filled by the lime green flowers of woodland hellebores.

Acer ginnala, a little tree, its leaves bright green (fleetingly scarlet in autumn) above creamy and fragrant panicled flowers, stands near a huge beech whose weeping branches cast a deeper shade over the lush greens of the moss and grass at its feet. Evergreen azaleas and camellias, _C. japonica_ and _C. williamsii_

Opposite: Gnarled boles of big woodland trees rise high above the flowering shrubs and allow enough light to reach them.

'Donation' among them, line one of the paths that lead from the main glade; another glade, curving gently, takes you to a grove of tall laburnums (*L.* × *watereri* 'Vossii'), a magnificent *Viburnum plicatum* 'Mariesii', and two enormous copper beeches, the ground beneath them washed over by an azure sea of bluebells. Where the rhododendrons have been thinned, primulas have sprung up – there is the fragrant yellow *P. florindae*, which seeds itself here and at the Castle of Mey, while another favourite of the Queen Mother's, *P. beesiana*, grows here and there and *P. denticulata*, the drumstick primula with flowers of lavender or white, flourishes in the damp woodland soil. There are all kinds of seedlings in the wood, showing how propitious are the conditions here for germination; I saw quantities of young *Rhododendron luteum* as well as some *Acer palmatum*, looking like a group of bonsai trees.

As we walked through the wood, the clear songs of birds rang out and in the pale palisade of birches I saw a long-tailed tit, its plumage perfectly matched to the powdery whites and charcoals of the trees. A green woodpecker flew from an immense sycamore (claimed by Mr Bond to be the finest specimen south of Doncaster), and somewhere a warbler sang.

The birds remind us of the importance of sound in a garden (as significant as sight, smell and touch) if we are to enjoy a full sensual experience. The odour of flowers and herbs, roses and honeysuckle, the texture of leaves and grasses and the velvet of buds, the sound of birdsong and running water, the contrasting shapes and colours of trees and hedges – all these must be present if the garden is to appeal to all the senses. Movement – the flight of bird, butterfly or bee, leaves falling, a wind bending the tops of trees or a breeze ruffling the petals of a flower – and light, that architect of all aspects of a garden, creator and sometimes destroyer, changing textures, enhancing colours, clarifying forms, combine to please both body and mind and give to the wanderer in the wood a vision of the ideal, a glimpse of paradise.

In this particular wood eyes, ears and nose are indeed enchanted – enchanted by magnolias and more magnolias: *M.* × *soulangeana nigra* and *M. rustica rubra*, their flowers rosy-claret and smelling of sweet lemons, two with creamy blossoms opening against the background of a copper beech, its young leaves a glistening curtain of amber and green. There is *Styrax japonica*, a small tree described by W. J. Bean as of 'singular grace and beauty', whose pure white flowers in June hang from delicate stalks like tiny lampshades, and another grove of rhododendrons. *R. praecox* is heavy with light and deep pink flowers and dark rose buds; *R. fortunei* (Chekiang China) is a magnificent species with huge white flowers, their centres flushed with green; near to this are the blood-red flowers and prominent calyces of *R. thomsonii* and the soft carmine of *thomsonii*'s less tender child, *R.* × *luscombei*. Perhaps most lovely of all is *R.* 'Hawk', a tall plant with abundant sulphur yellow flowers.

Left: There is something particularly lovely about the contrast between the abundant sulphur yellow flowers of the hybrid rhododendron 'Hawk' and the glossy dark green of its leaves.

Right: The very fragrant, lily-like flowers of the deciduous *Rhododendron luteum* (*Azalea lutea*), which grows freely at Royal Lodge.

Exploring the narrow side paths is a voyage of discovery. Leaving the broad glades to right and left, changing colours of moss and bright grass make vivid green ribbons that lead you into the woodland to yet more plantings of fine species rhododendrons and their hybrids. A particularly handsome hybrid, 'Norman Gill', which has large white flowers with a red blotch at their base, grows in the partial shade that it loves. This won an Award of Merit in 1922, and its breeding is 'Beauty of Tremough' × *griffithianum*. The acid Bagshot sand of this garden suits rhododendrons well, though a certain amount of organic fertilizer, mushroom compost and manure is used to encourage good growth and flowering – the Queen Mother does not like artificial fertilizer or chemical sprays to be used in the garden. I saw generous amounts of manure around the davidia trees, and Mr Bond is particular in seeing that they get this every year. The acid soil suits many other ornamental shrubs and trees and they have been freely planted. Among the cornus and sorbus I noted the uncommon *S. megalocarpa* with its red-purple young shoots and elegant foliage, a weeping birch (*Betula pendula* 'Youngii'), its branches graceful and drooping, its little leaves glittering in the uncertain sunlight. Revelling in the soil and light shade, *Pieris formosa* sports its shrimp-red young shoots, while an *Enkianthus campanulatus*, with pale creamy-pink flowers thick on the branches in May, has leaves that turn it into a burning bush of golden and red flames in autumn. *Hamamelis mollis*, the witch hazel, brightens the wood in February (or

Autumn brings an entirely new spectrum of colours and scents to the garden. The Queen Mother hopes to find the best of these on her return from Scotland at the end of October.

sometimes even earlier), when its bare twigs are covered with ragged yellow tufts of flowers exuding their pure, sweet-water scent, and later lily-of-the-valley covers a sweep of ground by an ancient wild rose.

Although, as Queen Elizabeth says, the garden at Royal Lodge is chiefly a spring and early summer one, the woodland is far from dull in late July and early August. The vibrant colours have faded, the greens have deepened and become lusher, and the tones are gentle – foxgloves and rosebay willowherb linger, *Hydrangea paniculata* is in full flower. That lover of moist and shady places, *Rodgersia pinnata* 'Superba', spreads its feathered and bronzed leaves out like

Enkianthus campanulatus does very well in the acid soil and light shade on the edge of the woodland garden. Its autumn colouring (*right*) is equally striking.

giant hands, a foot or more in width, its soft pink flowers on tall stalks. One rhododendron is still in flower, on the edge of the wood; it is the *R. auriculatum* hybrid 'Polar Bear'. Its young shoots are touched with a brilliant rose, and the white and highly scented flowers fill the air with fragrance as you pass.

Emerging from the woodland, we still have two parts of the garden to visit. One is to the east and can be entered from the gravelled forecourt, through the screen of trees I described earlier. We enter it now from the south, passing through a clump of *Acer palmatum*. Within this enclosure, formed by the trees and a rustic pergola on either side of it, stands 'The Little Cottage' ('Y Bwthyn Bach'), presented by the people of Wales in 1932 to Princess Elizabeth, the future queen, on the occasion of her sixth birthday.

Rambler roses, wisteria and honeysuckle clothe the pergola, and the beds beneath it are planted in spring with tulips and forget-me-nots. The white cottage is flanked by Irish yews, half covered in May with a *Clematis montana* that hangs in festoons and climbs high into the trees behind the cottage. A *Camellia saluensis* covered in pink flowers shows above the thatched roof, backed, among other trees, by a columnar *Chamaecyparis lawsoniana* 'Erecta', a conical *Thuja plicata*, and a *Phillyrea decora* with its dark and decorative leaves

49

forming billowing curves of deepest green. There is a white lilac too, and in front of the little cottage a formal garden is laid out, with four beds edged with a low clipped hedge of variegated euonymus (perhaps *E. fortunei* 'Variegatus'). These are planted with polyanthus, tulips and forget-me-nots, and later in the summer with miniature begonias in white, red and pink, interspersed with *Cineraria maritima*. By the side of the cottage there is a venerable rosemary, and old hybrid rhododendrons and *R. ponticum* form a screen of pinkish purple blossom to the right. Edging the paved path that leads to it from the forecourt are apricot and pink azaleas, a *Viburnum* 'Fulbrook' and rhododendrons *souliei* and *discolor* with rosy-white flowers. Later there will be hydrangeas in flower here, *H. serrata* 'Blue Bird' among them.

Close to the cottage, on its southern side, is the swimming-pool open to the southern sun yet skilfully sheltered by a group of silver birch trees and wild cherries, while at the pool's foot a huge wisteria grows on a tripod. Beyond it, and fringing the eastern side of the woodland garden, there is a wide informal border with plantings of ornamental trees, dwarf rhododendrons and hydrangeas, underplanted with a collection of narcissus including 'Suzy', 'Green Linnet' and 'Esmeralda'. The grass glade that leads up to the border is broad and closely mown, with, on the left, a grove of magnificent beeches with many ancient oaks and several fine Spanish chestnuts, planted in 1750, a year when many of the trees in Windsor Park were introduced. *Castanea sativa* is a tree known in England before the Norman Conquest and possibly introduced by the Romans; a faster-growing tree than the oak, it is very long-lived. Not long ago one was felled in Spain, to make way for a new road, and found to be over 1,000 years old. Queen Elizabeth's beloved magnolias have again been grown in plenty and in the border along the fringe of the woodland I see *M. liliflora* and *M. kobus* as well as *M.* × *loebneri* 'Leonard Messel' and *M. officinalis* 'Biloba', a magnolia from West China with a fig-like leaf. *Acer palmatum*, *Nyssa sylvatica*, and that delicious *Styrax hemsleyana*, with its yellow-anthered white flowers and grape-like velvety seed pods, are here too, as well as eucalyptuses, a *Clethra fargesii*, its flowers faintly scented, and an outstanding tree-like shrub, *Aralia elata* 'Variegata', the Japanese angelica tree, with its immense doubly pinnate leaves edged and marked with creamy white.

Our sight is bounded beyond the forest trees (the noble oaks, chestnuts and beeches) by a thick screen of *Rhododendron ponticum*, and beyond this is Windsor Park. Although a sharp eye is kept on it because it can be so invasive,

---

Opposite: This little cottage, too small for any adult to enter, has its own miniature formal garden. The cottage was given to the young Princess Elizabeth by the people of Wales, and has proved an endless source of pleasure to the Queen Mother's grandchildren and great-grandchildren.

Left: Mr Bennett, the head gardener at Royal Lodge, has been in Crown service for nineteen years. Until 1986 he was at the nearby Valley Gardens, gaining much experience of local soil and climate and of acid-loving plants such as rhododendrons.
Right: An aviary of budgerigars still stands in what was the Princesses' garden.

R. ponticum has been left in several places in the garden to form windbreaks for the more delicate shrubs and trees (and to provide pheasant cover). The garden is well-protected on the whole, but it is open to the west wind and the area is a fairly cold one.

The other part of the garden at Royal Lodge that we have not yet seen is the kitchen garden. To reach it we follow a gravel path that cuts across the lawns to the west, leaving the terrace on the right and below it a bed planted with 'Queen Elizabeth' and 'Fragrant Cloud' roses and a graceful group of *Acer palmatum* 'Trompenburg'. Queen Elizabeth does not grow much fruit or many vegetables because most of what she needs comes from the gardens at Windsor Castle; however, some special favourites can be found, mostly enclosed in cages to protect them from the depredations of the ubiquitous rabbit, and there is a long border growing flowers that can be cut for the house or to hold young plants used as replacements for the ornamental garden. *Thalictrum dipterocarpum* 'Hewitts Double' was looking wonderfully elegant with its tiny rosettes in clouds of pure lilac, and of course there are sweet peas – one of Queen Elizabeth's best loved flowers – to furnish bowls for her sitting-rooms and fill the house with a scent redolent of high summer.

There are two greenhouses, and they are filled with plants grown for the decoration of Royal Lodge – begonias, fuchsias and many different varieties of scented geraniums, their leaves smelling of nutmeg and lemon, rose and verbena, and a host of other exotic scents. The Queen Mother is especially fond of these and uses them a great deal in the house. Here again we can see her special feeling for scent, for besides the geraniums there are tender fragrant rhododen-drons in pots, including 'Lady Alice Fitzwilliam', and *Jasminum polyanthum*, a relation of *J. officinale*, but unlike it, needing the warmth of a greenhouse or conservatory. The flowers are in panicles of white with a blush of rose, the pink buds opening to an intensity of fragrance that will fill a room.

The kitchen garden is enclosed by hedges, and as you leave it, walking through a gateway in a beech hedge on the eastern side, and climb the gently rising slope towards the house, you pass a little graveyard in a corner by the terrace, where four of the Queen Mother's beloved corgis are buried. Their names, Jordie, Blackie, Honey Bee and Billy, are engraved on small and simple headstones.

It is to this house and garden, which must be so full of fond memories, that the Queen Mother comes to spend long weekends with her friends and family, surrounded by a peace and harmony so much of which she has herself created:

> *Those woven boughs, that silken sky*
> *Regret nor winter can come nigh;*
> *Beyond the reach of mortal grief*
> *Its every shining flower and leaf;*
> *Growing but fading not, shall be*
> *The span of its mortality,*
> *And time's sad progress shall be stayed*
> *By the perfection of a shade.*
>
> SYLVIA LYND

These lines seem to speak of the garden – its shadowy woodland, its bright flowers and flowing verdure – a garden where a King and his Queen worked together in partnership, marrying their creativity with that of nature to form a composition to gladden the heart and satisfy the senses, and which over the years has endured and blossomed under the knowledgeable and loving hand of Queen Elizabeth The Queen Mother.

Clarence House

LONDON

Should you be driving or walking down the Mall, leaving Buckingham Palace at your back, and were you to turn and glance to your left, you might catch (if you were sharp-eyed enough), through the fluttering leaves of a double avenue of plane trees, a glimpse of a house; an unusual house, and that is why you would note it, perhaps even slowing in your walk or your drive the better to observe it.

It is a large block of a house, standing out from its darker neighbours because of its attire of fresh and lively hues, the larger part the colour of a turtle dove's wing and the other parts a pearly bone. A wall rises beyond the outer line of plane trees, high and rather black, and you are aware of the low mass of St James's Palace to the right of the house. You know the wall must screen the garden of this building and you wonder what it is like. Does it have flower beds or a herbaceous border, and if so, what flowers and plants grow there? You know it has trees – fine trees – for you can see the full-foliaged tops of several rising high above the wall.

Your curiosity is kindled. You are a gardener and in London, and although gardening may be no part of your business at this moment, a gardener's thoughts easily return to their happiest subject of contemplation. Reflecting on this secret garden behind its high wall carries your fancy back to the time when all London seems to have been a garden bowered in green and rich in flowers.

In the days of Edward I, a nursery supplied gardener citizens with turf and flowering plants and trees; in 1140 the powerful Earl of Essex turned land he had

---

Opposite: Even without their leaves, the plane trees veil the garden with their intricate web of branches.

55

seized at Smithfield into a vineyard, and the gardens of the grand houses owned by the nobles swept down to the river. The palaces of the bishops had their gardens, and the dwellings of the rich merchants and even the houses of the poor had plots attached to them where they grew their own vegetables and flowers. As London grew, its gardens grew more and more numerous, and market gardens flourished to supply the city dwellers with fresh vegetables and fruit.

There were physic gardens as well as pleasure gardens, and herbers, like Queen Philippa's, planted thick with all the sweetest plants of the day. Orchards were richly stocked with plums and pears, quinces and cherries. One can imagine the foam of flower in the fields about the city, and showing above the walls of the plots; the apple trees clotted with blossom in spring and in autumn bending under the weight of fruit.

Later there were the grand gardens of Lambeth and Syon, famous for their roses, and those of the Temple, whose walks in the Great Garden were laid with cockleshells. In St James's Park, a cockle-strewer was appointed to look after the shell walks; this was in the reign of William and Mary, but even today in Queen Elizabeth's garden at the Castle of Mey there is a garden whose paths are strewn with shells.

In 1760 a visitor from Fulham found Lambeth to be 'a town of blooms and perfumes . . . the forecourt is quite fragrant with blossoms . . . jassamine clusters round the windows; the rose walk is today in its highest bloom. At every spot one moves to in the garden is some variety of sweets; here a gale of spicey pinks; there the breath of lilies . . .' The gardens great and small of the city of London move through your mind – from Ely and Lambeth, Hampton Court and Syon, the Great More House and the Temple, to Chelsea Hospital and Chiswick, Buckingham House and St James's Palace, and the myriad lesser delights besides, the little gardens tucked in between the walls of the houses, each inch of precious earth used to increase the pleasures and to satisfy the culinary needs of the people.

Who and what were the men who made these gardens? There were kings and queens, of course: Henry II and VIII, Henrietta Maria (the 'Rose and Lily Queen'), Charles II, William and Mary, and the Prince Regent. Sir William Temple with his famous garden at Sheen, John Evelyn and Sir Thomas More, the great Dr Turner ('The Father of English Botany'); Gerard with his garden at Holborn and the Tradescants with their nursery garden at Lambeth; Miller at Chelsea, Parkinson with his garden at Chelsea 'well-stocked with rarities', Kent and Brown, Repton and Robinson, they parade before us proclaiming their varied tastes – formal and informal, straight and serpentine, topiary and free-blowing trees – London has known them all, and has had her parks and gardens modelled by their skills as well as by the modes and fashions of the day.

56

The great formal gardens of Hampton Court in an eighteenth-century painting by Knyff.
London and the area around it has been rich with gardens for many centuries.

The fragrance of the herbers and orchards, the parks and trees, and the abundant flowers grown for the markets and sold from baskets in the streets of the city – violets and primroses, cowslips and lavender – comes floating back to us across the years.

'God Almighty first planted a garden. And indeed it is the purest of human pleasures,' wrote Francis Bacon. 'It is the greatest refreshment to the spirit of man; without which buildings and palaces are but gross handyworks.' Gross indeed were many of the handiworks as London expanded through the centuries, but still her citizens dug and planted, creating the new and guarding the old (for how doubly precious each green patch became), their husbandry bringing contentment to their spirits and with it a sense of security and relief.

It is with difficulty that you come back from these musings to the noise and fumes and traffic jams of modern London. However, possibly nothing today is noisier than the sound of the iron wheels of the carriages and carts on the rough and rutted paved streets of the city, or more odorous than the open sewers and the night-soil dropped from the windows of the houses into the streets below.

Left: The approach to Clarence House takes you past the towers and castellations of St James's Palace on your left.
Right: Marlborough House, like its close neighbour Clarence House, has been the London home of many members of the Royal Family over the years. This engraving shows it when it was the residence of Edward Prince of Wales.

The smells and sounds in those days were different, but were probably no less disagreeable to its people than are the fumes and roar of the motor car.

To know that there are today in the city of London more than 500 beekeepers is to paint a picture of an urban culture flowering in astonishing abundance. Indeed, the citizen of London is as fond of his garden as were his ancestors, and tends it with the same loving care, finding within its sheltering walls the harmony and peace he seeks as relief from the onerous life of the city. Queen Elizabeth The Queen Mother enjoys, like them, the oasis of her London garden, and it is from here that she works hardest, receiving visitors from home and abroad, entertaining friends, and, with her indomitable energy, supporting a host of charities.

Continuing your walk or drive down the Mall, your thoughts return once again to the present day. Turn left and you pass the towers and castellations of St James's Palace on the near side and the elegant architecture of Sir Christopher Wren's Marlborough House on your right. Another turn to the left brings you to the sentries on guard at the palace; a stamp, clank and rattle proclaim a presentation of arms. One more turn to the left and you are in a courtyard with Warwick House ahead of you, Stafford House (now Lancaster House) to your right, and to your left the pillars and gates of the painted house you glimpsed through the curtain of plane trees in the Mall.

The house is Clarence House, which has been the home of Queen Elizabeth The Queen Mother since 1953 when she moved here from Buckingham Palace with Princess Margaret. The entrance is one not unfamiliar to a number of people, either from photographs or in reality; for each year, on the Queen Mother's birthday on 4 August, these gates open and Her Majesty appears, surrounded by members of her family, to be greeted with flowers and good wishes by a happy throng of Londoners. At other times these gates open to receive carriages carrying heads of state, ambassadors, or kings and queens of foreign countries, calling on the Queen Mother to present their respects.

You move through these gates with their shiny black paint and wrought-iron lamps placed as finials on the gate-posts, the entrance set between dark blue

A call from the German Ambassador. Although a fine sight, it shows how the garden must play its role in the diplomatic activity of Clarence House. The lawns need constant attention because of the many visiting cars and carriages.

sentry boxes, and pass on into the garden . . . The gates close silently behind you and you find yourself by a large pillared portico, jutting out from the façade of the house. The portico's width is a little greater than that of a carriage and allows visitors to arrive and depart under the comfort of its sheltering roof.

Clarence House owes its name to the fact that it was built for the Duke of Clarence, afterwards William IV, and it has retained that name ever since. It was built on the site of the Duke's old lodgings, between Vanbrugh's Great Kitchen and Stable Yard, which had been given to him on his coming of age. Under the direction of Soane, much money was spent on these lodgings between the years 1791 and 1793, but the rooms were no more than a bachelor suite and when the Duke's mistress, Mrs Jordan, pressed for their redecoration and enlargement, sumptuous new furnishings were supplied. By 1811 the Lord Chamberlain's office had spent more than £13,000 on 'new chimney pieces, blue sarsnet hangings relieved by crimson panels', and elegant Grecian furniture.

It was in Clarence House that the King of Prussia and his sons took up residence during the visit of the allied sovereigns to this country in 1814, as did Prince Leopold of Saxe-Coburg before his marriage with Princess Charlotte in 1816. The public journals of the time tell us 'that so great was the throng of people anxious to see the Prince, that the footmen in letting him out of his

The Queen Mother is greeted by children who have waited for hours in the pouring rain outside Clarence House to give her gifts and cards on her eighty-fourth birthday.

Left: The Duke of Clarence, after he had become King William IV, in a portrait by M. A. Shee. Clarence House was built for him and his wife in the early nineteenth century.
Right: The 'amiable and excellent' Duchess of Clarence, later Queen Adelaide, painted by W. Beechey. She was the much-loved aunt of Queen Victoria.

carriage at Clarence House were nearly pushed under it, and that the pressure of the crowd was such that many persons were forced, against their will, within the walls'. This was of course before the portico was placed in its current position.

Despite Mrs Jordan's improvements, Clarence House was virtually rebuilt for the marriage of the Duke to Princess Adelaide of Saxe-Meiningen in 1818. Rooms which had satisfied a royal duke's mistress seemed no longer adequate for the use of a royal duchess in the 1820s, so in 1824 the Duke sought permission of George IV for alterations. 'His Majesty,' he wrote to Sir William Knighton, 'is fully aware of the inconvenience and unfitness of our present apartments here . . . I earnestly request, for the sake of the amiable and excellent Duchess, you will, when the King is quite recovered, represent the wretched state and dirt of our apartments.' Permission was given for the necessary work to be done, the Duke engaging John Nash to carry it out.

Nash was at this time busy planning and supervising considerable alterations to the adjoining Palace of St James, and he immediately drew up plans for this new enterprise. He proposed to convert the Duke's apartments into a plain three-storeyed house with attic and basement, the principal feature to be a portico in two storeys, the lower being of Doric order and the upper of Corinthian, projecting over the footpath to Stable Yard. Much of the old building was found to be in a far worse state than expected; Nash's original estimates, drawings and specifications had to be drastically revised and the house practically demolished before satisfactory rebuilding could be carried out. Costs steadily mounted, and the original estimate of £10,000 finally reached £22,000 when by the end of 1827 the carcass of the house was completed.

When the human and cheerful Duke of Clarence succeeded to the throne as William IV in June 1830, he showed marked reluctance to move to Buckingham Palace – he tried living in St James's Palace but the space was so limited that before a levée could be held the King and his Queen had to move all their books and papers out of the rooms. It was so inconvenient that before long a gallery, or passage of communication, was built on the first floor, connecting the rooms of the palace and Clarence House, and to this was shortly added a private entrance for the Queen. These improvements made it possible for the King to continue to live at Clarence House for some time after his succession.

William IV was a kind man and an indulgent brother and promised his sister Princess Augusta that he would improve her inconvenient lodging in Stable Yard between Clarence House on the north and Harrington House on the south. Harrington House stood on part of what is now the garden of Clarence House, and there were plans afoot at this time for pulling it down so that the Princess's residence could be enlarged. The Treasury, however, was unwilling 'to lay out money in enlarging an old house'. As a result, when the King died and Queen Adelaide removed to Marlborough House, Princess Augusta asked to be given Clarence House and remained there until her death in September 1840. We have in our mind a picture of her at a ball as a young girl, on a June evening in the year 1786. She was partner to her brother, the Duke of York, in a country dance when the Prince of Wales espied a certain Colonel Lennox who had that morning fought a duel with the Duke of York. Enraged and resenting bitterly the Colonel's presence among his sisters, the Prince broke up the ball. One can imagine the scene: the hot summer night, the graceful figures in rustling silks, the powdered hair, candles – their wax contorting in the heat – guttering and dripping, as the dancers moved through the lively figures of the rustic dance; then the drama of the Prince's arrival, his fury at the sight of – boldly dancing among his sisters – the man who had only that morning insulted his brother the Duke; the scattering guests, shocked and alarmed by the Prince's anger, the dying music.

A fine *Magnolia* × *soulangeana* dominates the view from the windows of Clarence House in spring.

The Princess lived only two short years at Clarence House, and it was then given by Queen Victoria to her mother, the Duchess of Kent. Before moving to Clarence House the Duchess had lived at Ingestre House in Belgrave Square, and she now removed the porch from there and had it erected at Clarence House. She also had a conservatory built at the end of Nash's great corridor, and the gallery linking the house with the state apartments converted into her wardrobe. Part of the garden front was exposed by the demolition of Princess Augusta's old lodgings, and this was stuccoed to match the rest of the building. The Duchess of Kent used Clarence House as her London home until she died in 1861; five years later, orders were given for Clarence House to be prepared as a home for Prince Alfred, Duke of Edinburgh, who was the second son of Queen Victoria and Prince Albert.

The house was extensively rebuilt for Prince Alfred, and during the year it took to complete these works, immensely solid foundations were discovered stretching far out on to the garden side of the Palace of St James. These were the foundations of Harrington House, and it was only with the greatest difficulty that the workmen were able to break them up. The years 1873 and

1874 saw further changes by the Duke of Edinburgh. A new wing and offices were added, the old portico and entrance opposite Stafford House were removed, and new ones were constructed on the side of the house facing St James's Park. This portico and entrance are the ones which are there to this day.

When the Duke of Edinburgh died in 1900, Queen Victoria's third son, the Duke of Connaught, used the house for forty-two years. When he died during the Second World War, in 1942, the house was handed over to the Red Cross and the St John Ambulance Brigade to become their headquarters. Two years later it once more became the home of a member of the Royal Family when Princess Elizabeth moved into the house. She lived there until her accession, when the Queen Mother moved to Clarence House and her daughter, the Queen, to Buckingham Palace.

Standing on the gravelled forecourt beside the Duke of Edinburgh's massive portico of 1874, looking out for the first time on the garden of Clarence House, you are immediately struck by two things. First, it seems much larger than you have imagined, perhaps because of the massive sweeps of lawn and the broad gravel paths which lead the eye to a noble stand of plane trees and beyond to another planting of trees, where your further view is obscured.

The raised walk, with the border behind showing its soldierly display of tulips and primulas in spring. The walk survives from the seventeenth-century garden designed by the great French gardener, André Mollet.

Clarence House is dwarfed by the great plane trees in the centre of the garden.

The other surprise of the garden is the raised walk on the southern side, ascended by two elegant flights of steps and bounded by a wall, that same wall that had blocked your view of the garden from the Mall. This walk seems to be the only feature remaining of the formal layout designed by André Mollet for Charles I's Queen, Henrietta Maria. The Queen brought Mollet over from France to design and plant the royal gardens, and on his first visit, from 1629 to 1633, he altered and re-laid out the gardens at St James's Palace. These were among the most important the great Baroque designer was to create in England, where he continued to work throughout the period of the Commonwealth.

In Mollet, Charles I and his Queen had found a master craftsman; one already well established, who also worked for Louis XIII of France and Queen Christina of Sweden. He was known far and wide, not only for his supremacy in garden design and planting but also for his book *Le Jardin de Plaisir*, which was translated into English in 1670. André was the youngest of three brothers, all trained by their father, Claude Mollet, who had designed and supervised the gardens of Henry IV of France. The influence of the Mollet family on garden design throughout a large part of Europe in the seventeenth century was very considerable, and André was perhaps the most influential of all – he travelled widely and introduced the family's skills, ideas and taste to those who were in the best position to be able to carry out his plans and designs.

Raised terraces such as the one remaining at Clarence House had not, however, been invented by the Mollets. Before their time, at least two important houses on the river Thames – Somerset House and its neighbour Arundel House – had them in their gardens. At Somerset House, raised walks about four steps high surrounded the symmetrical design of the garden (the garden was remodelled by Isaac de Caus for Anne of Denmark, James I's Queen), and the riverside terrace at Arundel House matches that at Somerset House. John Evelyn was later to have a raised walk in his garden at Wootton in Surrey.

How delightful it must have been to stroll along the finely sanded raised walks and be able to look down and admire the elaborate knots and patterns of

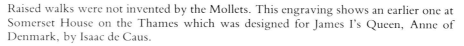

Raised walks were not invented by the Mollets. This engraving shows an earlier one at Somerset House on the Thames which was designed for James I's Queen, Anne of Denmark, by Isaac de Caus.

Part of the old Palace of St James overlooks the garden of Clarence House.

the parterres with their little hedges of box, or some other evergreen plant, either sinuously enclosing in an embroidery-like design the fashionable flowers of the day – auricula and damask rose, carnation and wallflower – or clipped more closely round coloured earths and sands.

The garden front at St James's Palace plays such an important part in the aspect of the garden at Clarence House as it is today, that it is interesting to imagine the gardens of previous centuries which would have been seen from the quarrelled windows of the Tudor palace, or from the tall sashed and astragalled windows of these rooms, their old crown glass glinting and winking in the light, shadowed or sunlit, of the different seasons.

St James's Palace was built between 1532 and 1540 as a hunting lodge for Henry VIII. It was a typical early Tudor building in the mixed style of Gothic and Renaissance architecture which characterized the age of its builder, with a majestic gateway and one large central court – 'a magnificent and goodly building' were the words used to describe it at the time.

We have a description of the building at this date from the time of Queen Elizabeth, by Norden, the Surveyor, who wrote:

> . . . not far from this glorious hall [Westminster Hall] another of Her Highnes houses descryeth itself, of a quadrate forme, erected of brick, the exterior shape where of, although it appears without any sumptuous or superfluous devices, yet is the spot very princelye, and the same with art contrived within and without. It standeth from other buildings almost two furlongs, having a farmhouse opposite to its north gate. But the situation is pleasant, indued with a good ayre and pleasant prospects. On the east London offereth itself to view; in the south the stately buildings of Westminster, with the pleasant park, and the delights there of; on the north the green fields.

As was the usual practice in those days, one that continued until at least the early years of the seventeenth century (Hatfield House in Hertfordshire, built in the years 1609–11, is an example), the palace was divided into a King's side and a Queen's side. The grounds were divided in a similar manner and these were walled, the east side being larger than the west – the Queen's side was to the west, probably where you can now see Clarence House. A description of what must have been the garden designed by André Mollet comes to us from Sieur de Serre: '. . . the other garden,' he writes, 'had divers walks, some sanded and others of grass, but both bounded on both sides by an infinity of fruit trees, which rendered walking so agreeable that one could never be tired.'

Growing in the garden of Clarence House today is an ancient mulberry (*Morus nigra*), which we shall look at more closely later; this could very possibly be one of the fruit trees mentioned by de Serre, for mulberries are long-lived trees. There is one growing in the west garden at Hatfield House, flourishing and fruiting in gnarled splendour, the only survivor of four planted by James I, who brought quantities of trees into the country with the intention of starting a silk industry in England. Unfortunately the King was ill-advised and the black mulberry (*Morus nigra*), which is not relished by the silkworm, was the one introduced. The King's enterprise therefore went unrewarded; however, as a result of it we have some very fine old mulberry trees in this country.

Clarence House garden is surely the one described by de Serre, and which we can see in the extract from Faithorne and Newcourt's map, surveyed in 1643–7 and published in 1658. This shows a large rectangular parterre, with a smaller one before the south front of the palace, both within an enclosure which looks much the same size as that of the garden to be seen at Clarence House today, and with what appears to be a raised walk on the southern side.

Opposite: The black mulberry, as illustrated in John Evelyn's *Sylva* of 1662. The venerable specimen in the garden at Clarence House may well date from about this time.

The ♀ Mulberry Tree.

John Miller del. et Sculp.

Publish'd Jan.ʳ 1ᵗ 1776. by A. Hunter M. D. as the Act directs

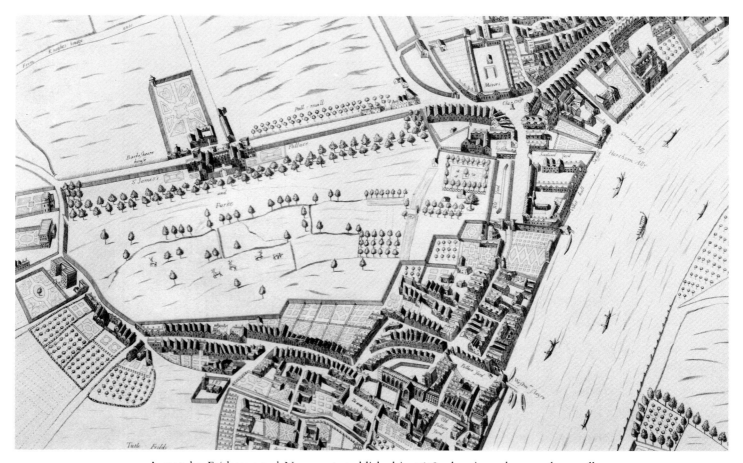

A map by Faithorne and Newcourt, published in 1658, showing a large and a small parterre beside St James's Palace. These cover an area which seems about the same size as Clarence House's garden.

During the last years of the Interregnum St James's Palace had become a barracks and military headquarters, and on the eve of the Restoration it was occupied by troops under the command of General Monck, but there appears to be evidence that as soon as the Restoration was a certainty, preparations were made to make the palace fit for royal use. There is a painting of the palace of *c.* 1690 showing the garden front, and at the time of the Restoration it was given to the Duke and Duchess of York as their residence. A great deal of money was spent on doing up the apartments, which were described at the time as having been 'very nobly trimmed up for their occupation'. Indeed, a French visitor considered that the Duke and Duchess were 'better lodged than the King and Queen'.

The raised walk is shown enclosing the three sides of the garden, the southern side ascended by one flight of steps in the centre, and the east and west walks with flights of steps on their northern ends. The steps to the southern walk are approached by a broad sanded path, lined on either side by what appear to be vases on plinths, alternating with formal trees which may or may not be

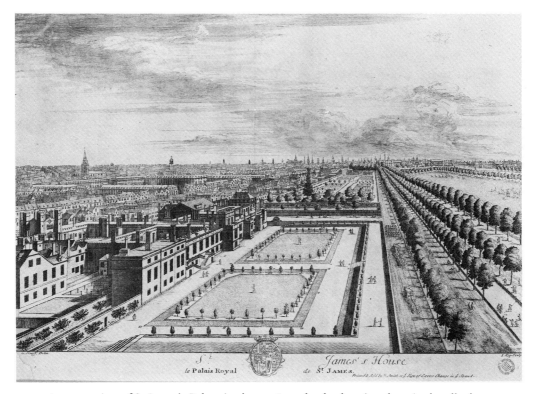

An engraving of St James's Palace in about 1690, clearly showing the raised walk along the Mall looking very much as it does today. Clarence House now stands where you can see fruit trees neatly pruned against the wall.

clipped. All along the northern edge of the raised walk are vases with plants in them, and in an engraving of the same date the large rectangles, which the central path divides, are shown as being surrounded by small trees; the rectangles themselves seem to be grass knots or simple grass sward, and one cannot see any sign of a parterre de broderie.

Later engravings, made during the early years of the eighteenth century, also show a great many small trees formally surrounding rectangles of sward that are viewed from the height of the raised walks, these also being edged with trees. Can these be the fruit trees described with such enthusiasm by de Serre? Certainly fruit trees can be seen in one of these engravings, neatly pruned against the south-facing wall running from the west end of the garden front of the palace, where Clarence House now stands.

When Charles II returned from exile in France he brought with him a passion for a game called 'palle maille', a kind of croquet played in an allée, and thereupon built the royal 'palle maille' allée in St James's Park. Finding that the traffic disturbed his game, he moved the road to the north in 1631, re-naming

it Catherine Street; it is now known as Pall Mall, and is today one of the approach roads to Clarence House. Moving this road made the land on the left and right of St James's Palace attractive for development, and Nell Gwyn, as well as other notable figures of the time, built fine houses overlooking the park and were then able to be near the King and watch him playing his games.

A century later, in the year 1769, a plan of the bailiwick of St James's shows what is now the garden of Clarence House, looking little changed. The raised walks are still there, although the approaches of the eastern and western flights of steps have been altered, and you mount them facing east or west, instead of towards the south. However, the rectangles seem to be surrounded by small trees, and these are now joined together by hedging with entrances; and the central layout of the rectangles has been changed to a lozenge shape with the same trees and hedges outlining the design. By this time the influence of the landscape school on the development and creation of parks and gardens was widely felt; parterres and topiary were being swept away, straight lines were becoming the curving, sinuous ones of nature, and any formality was unacceptable to the fashionable opinions of the day.

Strangely enough the Clarence House garden seems to have escaped the 'landscaper's' attentions, although in a painting of 1827, showing the garden front of the palace, trees have been allowed to grow in a naturalistic manner, almost forming a shrubbery which screens the lower windows. By 1829, however, these trees have once more been brought under control in a most unfashionable manner, framing hedged enclosures in the old rectangular shape, the only change and apparent concession to informality being several trees planted haphazardly within the enclosures. They, of course, could be the remaining trees from the earlier formal planting.

It is even more strange that Clarence House garden retained its formality when you see on the same plan of 1829 three gardens, in close proximity to it, all of which are laid out in the 'naturalistic' style, with winding paths sinuously curving through what appear to be shrubs and trees – perhaps the Duke of Clarence and his Duchess did not favour the new trends in garden design, though lack of interest or lack of money may well have been the main reason that changes were not made in line with the fashions of the day. The Duke was a careful man. The example of the excesses and extravagances of his brother George IV, who with Nash as his architect was developing Marylebone Park (soon to become Regent's Park), building a pagoda and bridge in St James's Park, and creating Carlton House, may have led the Duke to exercise a greater restraint in money matters. For whatever reason, the Clarence House garden

---

Opposite: The plane's branches form a canopy of shade. Leaves drop throughout the summer, making sweeping a constant task for the gardener.

A large classical portico, built by Prince Alfred and seen here in the very early morning, allows visitors to alight in the dry.

did not become a 'naturalized' one, although there are elements in it today which make it plain that it has not entirely escaped the influence of Nash, his partner Repton, and their immediate predecessors.

In spite of some changes in the garden, both John Nash and André Mollet might feel a little at home there today, or would at least be able to recognize some solid remains of their style. Nathaniel Cole too, the author of *Royal Palaces and Gardens*, published in 1827, might be surprised to see traces of the new taste in gardens that he had introduced in the nineteenth century – the elaborate 'Victorian' bedding-out and bright colour schemes. If the ghosts of all three should walk in the garden today, they would no doubt be puzzled by what they saw, but there would certainly be elements in the layout and the planting which they could each acknowledge as their own.

As we stand before the portico on this spring day in April, it is interesting for us to see how little changed are the bones of the garden from those of its earliest days. The raised walks on the east and west sides of the enclosure have gone, it is true, and there is a small lodge by the gravel drive and gates opening on to the Mall, which divides the raised walk on the south. The walk now carries a border along its whole length, small trees have become full-foliaged giants, beds have been cut in turf here and there, and young trees planted – but the framework of the garden remains largely unaltered. Stepping from the shadow of the great portico, however, into the fitful sunlight of this early spring morning, you notice immediately plants and flowers that proclaim the taste of Queen Elizabeth The Queen Mother – for it is distinct and very personal and makes each of her gardens peculiarly her own.

The first of these that you are aware of is a rectangular bed of hyacinths cut in the vivid green turf in front of the portico and running along the east-facing wall of the garden. It is packed with hyacinths, 800 of them, bulb against bulb, their flowers a *mélange* of pale pink and pale blue. John Parkinson, writing in his *Paradisus Terrestris* in 1629, says that 'all these oriental hyacinths . . . have been brought out of Turkie, and from Constantinople, but where their true original place is is not yet understood . . . they abide a great while in flower in great beauty especially if the weather be milde, when as few or no other flowers at that time are able to match them'.

Queen Elizabeth likes the hyacinths to be in two blues, a light and a darker one; 'Myosotis' and 'King of the Blues' would have been her choice, but this particular year pink impostors have appeared. Nevertheless they are an effective sight, and as you look down at them their unique scent is carried up to your expectant nose.

It is a scent at once penetrating yet sweet and delicate, with a touch of wallflower and stock, admirably described by Shelley in 'The Sensitive Plant':

> *And the hyacinth purple, and white, and blue,*
> *Which flung from its bells a sweet peal anew*
> *Of music so delicate, soft, and intense,*
> *It was felt like an odour within the sense . . .*

These plants at Clarence House are the florist's hyacinths, bred chiefly by Dutch raisers in great variety, from *Hyacinthus orientalis*; the original plant is found growing among limestone rocks, high in the hills of Turkey and Syria, Persia and the Lebanon, and was introduced into England in 1560 by Anthony Jenkinson.

It is a flower of myth and classical romance – Greek fable tells of the fatal love of Phoebus Apollo, the god of the sun, the shining one, for the beautiful youth Hyacinth, son of a Spartan king; Phoebus' love was returned, but Zephyr too loved Hyacinth, and in a fit of jealous rage he flung Apollo's quoit at the youth's head, killing him. From his blood, spilt by the avenging Wind, sprang the flower that carries his name.

For Elizabethans as well they were sad flowers: 'the melancholy hyacinth' they called it, its shadowed spikes of purple-blue associated by them, as well as violets, with sadness, the fable doubtless affecting their feeling for the flower. However, it has happy associations too; in Greece, crowns of hyacinth were worn by maidens at weddings, and Homer claims that with other flowers, it helped to form the couch of Juno:

> *And clustering Lotus swell'd the rising bed,*
> *And sudden hyacinths the turf bestrow*
> *And flow'ry Crocus made the mountain glow . . .*

The bed where the hyacinths are actually planted, in the square of lawn that abuts directly on to the porch, needs humus and water, as it is only six feet above the cellars of the house and therefore dries out rather easily. The humus is supplied by horse manure from the Horse Guards, and an application of peat. Later in the summer the bed is packed with fuchsias; some are low bushy plants, others rise above their fellows as small standards supported by canes and these give height to the centre of the bed. They are a riot of pale and deep pinks, whites and rosy reds, and interspersed with them are plants of the spicy-sweet scented heliotrope.

The fuchsia, that plant of conservatories, bedding-out and the cottage window, much loved by the Victorians (its flowers even look a little like a lady in a crinoline), was discovered at the end of the seventeenth century by French botanist Jean Plumier, who had been sent on three voyages to the West Indies by Louis XIV, in 1689, 1693 and 1695. Except for two that are found in New Zealand, fuchsias are indigenous to Mexico, Chile and Peru and only arrived in Britain at the end of the eighteenth century. There are some fifty species and almost all of them, and their cultivars, will do well in the open air in the summer months. Some will even flourish without protection in winter if they are treated like herbaceous plants, while one or two quite tender species can be grown successfully in mild areas, if trained against a sheltering wall. Two species, *F. coccinea* and *F. magellanica*, were first brought to Europe by the French plant collectors, and the latter is the hardy parent of scores of hybrids – it is the one which grows with such charming vigour and abandon in the south and west of Ireland, framing Irish cabin windows and forming the hedges that billow in a haze of scarlet along many an Irish roadside and boreen. It flourishes, too, in Devon and Cornwall, and in Wales and the west Highlands. There is a story of a Mr James Lee, a nurseryman in Hammersmith and already owner of the two species, who saw a fuchsia plant in a pot in the window of a lady's cottage in

Left: Graceful *Fuchsia magellanica*, one of the first species to be introduced to Europe from South America and the hardy parent of scores of hybrids.
Right: Planted among the fuchsias in an appropriate Victorian mixture is the delicious *Heliotropium peruvianum*. Its heady scent of cherries reaches far into the garden.

Wapping. He thought this plant fairer than either of the others, and determined then and there to possess it. At first nothing could persuade the good lady to part with it, her husband, a sailor, having brought it to her. However, after a good deal of haggling, Lee persuaded her to sell the plant to him for eight guineas, and without more ado, he set to work to strike as many cuttings as he could; soon he had 300 plants which he sold at a guinea each – launching in this way the fashion for fuchsias and a fortune for himself.

One of the hardiest of all fuchsias was raised at Riccarton near Edinburgh in 1850 and named *F. riccartonii*. A cross between *F. magellanica* and *F. corallina*, it has the brightest of flowers which it produces abundantly, dropping like little scarlet flames drenching the foliage. All through the summer and autumn, it is this variety and *F. magellanica* which grow so happily and vigorously at the Castle of Mey, flaming against the grey walls of the garden there. Planted among the fuchsias here, as we have already noted, is the delicious heliotrope – *Heliotropium peruvianum* – so called because its flowers, like those of the sunflower, which the French call 'Tournesol', follow the sun. It came to this country from Peru before 1757, via France where it is a native, and it is suitable that it should be planted among the fuchsias in this bed because it, too, was loved by the Victorians, and like the fuchsia grows in southern Ireland, forming great hedges in districts where the Gulf Stream creates a mild climate. It scents the air for miles around – the smell is of freshly baked cherries cooked in a pie, hence the charming country name of 'Cherry Pie' by which it is commonly known. The flowers bloom in clotted clusters – shading from the palest lavender to the deepest purple, a colour redolent of the nineteenth-century taste in fashion.

The modern hybrids are not worth a fig – all the charm has been bred out of them. The scent has nearly gone, the flower clusters are too big and the colours unsubtle. The only one to bother with is the old well-loved favourite from Peru – it is said to be useful too, its flowers providing a tincture that is good for warts and sore throats; besides which, should you have such a fancy, the plants can be made into standards, every side-shoot being taken off the stem to the chosen height. After a few years the stem will have become a considerable trunk, carrying bushy heads covered with flowers which last well indoors and will fill a whole room with their spicy sweetness.

This is the plant Queen Elizabeth loves, the one that reminds her of her childhood, for it was grown by her mother, Lady Strathmore, in the gardens of her home at Glamis Castle in Scotland, its heady scent and old-fashioned look being an especial joy to her.

Another plant used in this bed with the fuchsias and the heliotrope, a good foil for them and popular in the same era, is *Chlorophytum elatum variegatum*. It has an unusual way of increasing itself, sending out long side-shoots with babies on them, the ends rooting where they touch down. The plant's common name is 'spider plant' because of this curious habit.

As we saw at Royal Lodge, a further great favourite of the Queen Mother is the magnolia, and there are several specimens planted by Her Majesty in the garden at Clarence House; one is the hybrid *M. × soulangeana*, which grows in a graceful spreading shape in the sward of a second sweep of lawn we have reached by crossing a gravel path running east and west. It is in full flower for this April visit to the garden, its goblet-shaped blooms, white inside and a delicate pale purple outside, thickly covering the naked shoots of the tree. This hybrid was raised by Soulange-Bodin in Paris; it was a cross between *M. denudata* and *M. liliflora*, and first flowered in 1826. It will live to a great old age, and can eventually reach 20 feet, being especially happy in London where it enjoys the rather acid soil and warmer conditions, untroubled by pollution because of its deciduous nature.

The magnolia is the only tree or shrub with such large single flowers that can survive out of doors in temperate regions, and very beautiful and spectacular it is, some species having immense leaves that need a sheltered spot if they are to survive undamaged.

In the grass beneath the *Magnolia × soulangeana*, and encircling it, are quantities of purple and white crocus. These are Dutch hybrids, mostly

The handsome goblet flowers of *Magnolia* × *soulangeana*. The tree is particularly happy
in London, where it enjoys the slightly acid soil and warmer conditions.

descended from *C. vernus*, and they were planted by Queen Elizabeth to
coincide with the flowering of the magnolia; the effect is as pretty as an iced
cake, a mound of creams and pinks wreathed in sugared violets. To the west and
on our right there is a large flower bed jutting forward into the lawn, its edges
cut into rounded curves and rising fairly steeply towards the raised walk. This
high piece of ground must be all that remains of the east-facing raised walk
created by André Mollet. The front of this bed is planted out in the spring with a
mass of red tulips called 'Diplomat' (900 of them!), to be followed in the
summer by the scarlet geranium 'Sprinter' (*Pelargonium* × *hortorum zonale*)
which had to replace 'Gustave Emich', successful for many years but which
finally developed black leg, a disease difficult to eradicate. Queen Elizabeth
expresses great affection for these geraniums, plants which are, like the fuchsia
and the heliotrope, fondly remembered from her childhood days.

A brilliant mass of *Pelargonium* 'Sprinter' can be seen from the drawing-rooms of Clarence House in the summer, reminding the Queen Mother of her childhood at St Paul's Waldenbury.

Behind this spring and summer bedding-out, and forming a firm background to it, are several shrubs. There is *Mahonia* 'Charity', a fine evergreen, flowering in the saddest months of the year, November and December, with deep yellow flowers in racemes that spread outwards and upwards. The plant was one of three chosen by Sir Eric Savill from seedlings growing in L. R. Russell's nursery in Surrey which had originated from the Slieve Donard Nursery in Co. Down, the seed parent being *M. lomarifolia* and the pollen parent the lily-of-the-valley-scented *M. japonica*. This stately shrub (the original one in the Savill Gardens is 14 by 12 feet), together with some bushes of *Griselinia littoralis* (that plant with thick and shiny apple-green leaves that thrives in sea-air) and an ancient *Clematis montana* draped in garlands along the corner of the south and east walls and trailing over the shrubs in the bed, form with their varying greens an excellent

A fine evergreen shrub, *Mahonia* 'Charity' brightens the garden in November and December with its yellow flowers.

background to two more magnolias. These are varieties of *M. × soulangeana*, one called 'Lennei' and the other 'Gander', both planted by Queen Elizabeth. 'Lennei' was presented to the Queen Mother by the Irish Society and grows 10–15 feet in height. It was born in Italy, but where it was raised is not certain; Van Houtte, writing of it in *Flore des Serres* (1693), said it was the gift of the 'charming little bees of Lombardy', another tradition claims that it was raised in Vicenza in 1850, and still another that Count Giuseppe Salvi raised it in Florence naming it 'Maometto' (Mahomet). But whatever tale is the truth, it is an extremely beautiful hybrid with several advantages over the average forms of *M. × soulangeana*. First, the flowers are finer and more richly coloured – rosy-purple outside, white within, the petals shaped like broad spoons; second, the tree occasionally bears another crop of flowers in the autumn; and third, as the spring flowers do not appear until late in April and throughout May, they often remain uninjured by frost.

Frost is no great problem in this garden, causing little damage during the winter months. Indeed, almost a micro-climate prevails; the garden is a sun-trap, its aspect is southern, it is surrounded by walls and therefore is warm and sheltered. To do well, all plants need sun and a free circulation of air, and while almost all town gardens suffer from a lack of these, this is not the case at Clarence House. This is fortunate indeed, as it means the climate is not a limiting factor in the selection of plants.

Atmospheric pollution is a much less serious problem than it used to be in the days of the coal fire, and since the passing of the Clean Air Act in 1956 it has become possible to grow a wider selection of plants in the city. No longer does soot collect on leaves and stems, clogging the pores through which the plants breathe, and evergreens now do quite well in London. However, fumes from traffic and factories are still a problem, and acid and sulphur as well as lead are very injurious to plant life.

Climbing the flight of stone steps on to the raised walk and turning to look down, as others have done in earlier centuries, on the scene below us, our eye takes in the massive sweeps of lawn, the broad gravel walks, immaculately raked, and a noble stand of plane trees (*Platanus* × *hispanica acerifolia*), their branches sweeping like green curtains to the ground. These are the lawns that Queen Elizabeth loves – loving too their daisies and moss – and indeed, on a summer's day, of what account is a lawn without daisies, the sprinkled white intensifying the green of the shining grass? How poorly childhood would be served if there were no daisies for necklace, coronet and chain to be woven, seated on the sweet-smelling turf in the warmth of the sun. Lawn perfectionists may well shudder at these sentiments, but the memory sustains affection for them.

'Nothing is more pleasant to the eye than green grass finely shorn,' wrote Francis Bacon, and how right he was. Queen Elizabeth has had extra turf inserted along the edges of the paths to shrink their width as much as the passage of a carriage will allow, much disliking gravel and wishing to increase the grassed area as much as possible. Nevertheless, these gravel paths are a practical necessity because of the cars and carriages that make their way into the garden, bearing the Queen Mother's guests. Coming in by one gate, they circle the lawns and go out at another, also in the west wall of the garden.

Loved too are the great planes whose swelling heads of green dominate the whole garden. Coming out late in the year and dropping early, they shade the hot summer days but let light penetrate the garden in the dark of winter. Even when leafless they are decorative, the giant burr-like fruits hanging in chains from the web of branches until spring.

The Queen Mother enjoys the cool green shade of her plane trees.

A poem by Amy Levy called 'A London Plane Tree' emphasizes what an exceptionally lovely tree this was when others were badly affected by pollution, before the Clean Air Act was passed:

> *Green is the plane tree in the square,*
> *The other trees are brown;*
> *They droop and pine for country air;*
> *The plane tree loves the town.*
>
> *Here from my garret-pane I mark*
> *The plane tree bud and blow,*
> *Shed her recuperative bark,*
> *And spread her shade below.*
>
> *Among her branches, in and out,*
> *The city breezes play;*
> *The dull fog wraps her round about;*
> *Above, the smoke curls grey.*
>
> *Others the country take for choice,*
> *And hold the town in scorn;*
> *But she has listen'd to the voice*
> *On city breezes borne.*

The London plane is a tree of mysterious origins. It is not known how it is bred, where it came from or when it was introduced, although a date of 1663 has been given. The size of living specimens suggests that it must have been in cultivation by the middle of the eighteenth century – there is a huge one at Kew which is thought to date from 1773, when the gardens were laid out by 'Capability' Brown. Queen Elizabeth thinks that her trees must be about 150 years old, and this would tally with the major changes made to the house by the Duke of Clarence.

Perhaps the London plane is a form of *Platanus orientalis*, or a hybrid between this and *P. occidentalis*. G. Berry writes about the London plane in *The Garden* in 1887; he calls it the 'Western Plane' but his comments are no less true:

> As a rule the Western Plane thrives better in and about London than any other park tree; consequently it has been planted extensively there during the present century, and has succeeded so well that it has become known throughout the country under the appellation 'London Plane'. In the numerous squares and gardens it is certainly surprising to see how healthy, clean and fresh-looking this Plane appears . . . Although surrounded by myriads of chimneys, its leaves for size and freshness can vie almost with the foliage of trees in the country, far removed from smoke and town atmosphere. This Plane seems particularly well adapted for smokey towns on account of the smooth glossy surface of the leaves and their light green colour, and also the shedding of its bark, which gives the stem such a healthy, clean look.

In summer the Queen Mother makes good use of what she calls her 'salles vertes'. Guests are entertained to lunch under the graceful hanging branches.

Queen Elizabeth loves the canopy her planes create; their branches drop and fall, cascading like a verdant cataract to the ground, their tips caressing the grass and forming the 'court rooms' that her Majesty calls her 'salles vertes' – 'There the "salon" and there the "salle à manger" ' – where chairs and sofas are set and a table spread; they are much used when the weather is fine enough. The privacy is complete, the tapestries of verdure forming the walls of the 'rooms', screening all from outside gaze. Once there was a gap in the billowing screen, but this was filled by the planting of sweet almond trees and autumn-flowering cherries, so protecting Queen Elizabeth's privacy still further from the windows of Lancaster House. On grey November days the cherry's semi-double white and blush flowers are a delight, or on any grey winter's day from then to March. Like the pyrus, the prunus are good Londoners and flower particularly well in the city, cheering the heart at a time when spring seems so very far away.

The planting up of the gap in the group of planes was the idea of Mrs Bennie White, the recently retired gardener at Clarence House, who worked in the garden there for 26½ years; now in her retirement, she travels the world. A character known to everyone as 'Bennie', with a passion for poetry and the solitary pursuits of music and gardening, her heart is still much engaged in the garden at Clarence House, and it is clear that she misses it a great deal. Each year on the Queen Mother's birthday she buys a bunch of all the flowers she knows Queen Elizabeth loves the most and sends them to Her Majesty at Clarence House, and when, during the time she was gardening there, the sweet black grapes from the vine growing in the great lead cistern (1729) against the wall of the palace were ripe, she would pick them and send them to Queen Elizabeth in Scotland. This vine was a cutting from a plant grown at 11 Downing Street; a grape called the 'Hanover Black Grape', small and very sweet. However, no reference can be found for this, so it seems more likely to be the 'Black Hamburg', which was a vine introduced from Hamburg in the eighteenth century, quickly becoming very popular. Ripening in October, it can be made into wine and is a good grape for cold greenhouses, the gigantic and famous vine at Hampton Court being this same variety.

The lead water cistern where the Clarence House vine grows is marked generously with graffiti, a relic of the days when the soldier guarding the palace passed this way on sentry duty (now he has been replaced by more sophisticated, but less romantic, security techniques). In the summer time the vine it contains is underplanted with deep pink ivy-leaved geraniums and pink petunias which trail gracefully and spill over the top of the cistern, its dull leaden hue a perfect foil for their brilliance.

Turning away from the contemplation of the garden below us we continue our stroll on the raised walk, whose whole length carries a broad border broken only by another pair of gates and the lodge now used by the gardener, to which you descend by steps. The border on the walk is filled with many of the Queen Mother's favourite flowers, and very special attention is given to the areas that can be seen by Queen Elizabeth from her bedroom window, these being planted with the plants she likes the most. So as to have good colour throughout the spring and summer a great deal of bedding-out of annuals is done; there are quite a number of perennials as well, and although they are not as numerous as they used to be, many having died out, they are now being divided up and added to again.

A fruiting grapevine, grown from a cutting taken at 11 Downing Street, shares the great lead cistern (1729) with an attractive mixture of ivy-leaved pelargoniums, nicotiana and *Helichrysum petiolatum*.

On this spring day polyanthus make gay patches of yellow in the forefront of the border. This flower, which was grown with such passion and dedication in the nineteenth century by flower-fanciers in Lancashire and Cheshire, is a cross between the primrose and cowslip. Many varieties were grown in the seventeenth century, and in 1770 the Reverend William Hanbury was to write, when advising that they should be raised from seed, '. . . you have a treasure upon the ground of which you do not know the value . . . more than a thousand varieties of Polyanthas have I had at one blow in a single bed', but it was not until 1880, when Miss Gertrude Jekyll found a plant with yellow flowers growing in her garden, that a polyanthus of this colour appeared.

Out at the same time as the polyanthus is the scarlet Darwin tulip 'Diplomat', together with blue *Muscari armeniacum*, the grape hyacinth. Ruskin wrote of this flower that it was 'as if a cluster of grapes and a hive of honey had been distilled and pressed in one small boss of celled and beaded blue'. Various daffodil hybrids also enliven the scene, and later the summer bedding arrives, supplied like the bulbs by the Department of the Environment through the Royal Parks. Everything has to be planted by the day of Trooping the Colour, which is a key day for the garden at Clarence House, a high point of the year, when all has to be in good order for the entertaining Queen Elizabeth does at that time. There are of course other special events, and the gardener is supplied with a schedule so that the gardening can be done to fit these occasions.

Among the bedding plants set out in this great border are cannas (*C. hortensis*), first planted in this country in the seventeenth century, salvias (*S. splendens*), and *Alyssum maritima*, the latter growing 6–10 inches high and used in this country as an annual, though it is more strictly a perennial. Alyssum is the rather despised plant used to supply the 'white' in a patriotic colour scheme with blue lobelia and scarlet salvias, but it can be delightful planted in a snowy carpet on its own, strongly scenting the air with its sweet pervasive smell. Here too is *Cleome spinosa*, a plant from tropical America introduced in 1817; its common name is the 'spider flower', and it is thought of by Queen Elizabeth as essentially a London plant, so seldom is it seen used outside the capital. Of course here too are more generous plantings of Her Majesty's favourite *Heliotropus peruviana*.

No calceolarias or African marigolds (*Tagetes erecta*) are grown, as the Queen Mother dislikes them, but there are large patches of the short-growing *Nicotiana hybrida* in mixed colours; scentless, their flowers remain open all day unlike the old *Nicotiana alata* syn. *affinis* (a perennial in its native Brazil), whose flowers close in the day to open at night and fill the evening air with scent. Tall notes in the border are large groups of the roses 'Queen Elizabeth' and 'Peace' – the former was raised in the USA in 1954 by Dr Lammerts and is a cross between 'Charlotte Armstrong' and 'Floradora'; 'Peace', perhaps one of the most famous roses in the world, was raised by Meilland in France, its parents being 'George Dickinson' and 'Souvenir de Claudius Pernet'. Both these roses are suited to hard pruning, for they are coarse growers; 'Peace', though, may produce blind shoots if too severely cut, but these will break eventually and flower later. Its flowers are lemon yellow flushed with pink and very large; those of 'Queen Elizabeth' are a clear pink, both single and in trusses. Here at Clarence House the plants are more than twenty years old but are nevertheless most determined flowerers – especially 'Queen Elizabeth' – and there is rarely a month when they do not show some colour.

Also growing in this border are some *Iris germanica* hybrids and hemerocallis or day lilies, all un-named varieties. These are permanent features, along with a plant of *Ceratostigma plumbaginoides* at the front of the border. This was discovered, like so many other good plants, by Ernest Wilson in West China, and brought home in 1906. It is a dwarf shrub about a foot high, whose leaves

The floribunda rose 'Queen Elizabeth' is exceptionally vigorous and disease-free, and at Clarence House grows in a clump over 4 feet high. Beautifully shaped clear pink blooms make it perfect for cutting and compensate for its rather leggy appearance in the border.

A useful shrub planted at the front of the herbaceous border: *Ceratostigma plumbaginoides*.

and stems turn a lovely glowing red late in the year and whose flowers are a brilliant blue and continue to appear till very late in the autumn. The front of the border used to run in a perfectly straight line, but two years ago Bennie White, with the agreement of Queen Elizabeth, gave it a scalloped edge in an effort to reduce formality and to arrive at a more 'natural' and soft effect.

These plantings have one of the finest of all backgrounds for flowers, a holly hedge, which is planted against the wall fronting the Mall – the same wall on which Queen Adelaide had held the young Princess Victoria while watching her husband William IV's first opening of Parliament. The hedge is formed of *Ilex aquifolium*, the common holly – the darkest of dark greens, glittering, impenetrable, it is a native of this country and has been cultivated for centuries.

The Tudors and Stuarts doted on holly, clipping it into strange shapes in their knot gardens and parterres, loving especially the variegated sorts with the particoloured leaves of silver and gold, which in the eighteenth century were known by delicious names such as 'Fine Phyllis Holly', 'Painted Lady Holly', and 'Glory of the East'. But of all admirers of the holly hedge, John Evelyn was the greatest, constantly exhorting his friends to plant them: '. . . is there under heaven,' he writes in his *Sylva*, 'a more glorious or refreshing object of this kind than an impregnable Hedge, which I can show in my poor garden at any time of the year glittering with its armed and varnish of leaves? The taller standards at orderly distances, blushing with their natural coral. It mocks the worst assaults of the Weather, Beasts and Hedgebreakers . . .'

Evelyn had written in his diary of 1 May 1683, 'I planted all the out-limites of the garden and long walks with holly', and his finest hedge, planted in 1670, was 400 feet long, 9 feet high, and 5 feet in diameter, a truly remarkable specimen. But alas! impenetrable as Evelyn claimed it to be, it was not proof against the antics of Peter the Great, Czar of Russia, who having rented Sayes Court from John Evelyn in 1698, when he came to England to learn shipbuilding, had himself, as a morning exercise, trundled through the famous hedge in a wheelbarrow. Evelyn in his diary mourns 'my now ruined garden at Sayes Court (thanks to the Czar of Moscovy). I went to Deptford to see how miserably he had left my house after three months making it his Court. I got Sir Christ. Wren, the King's Surveyor and Mr London his gardener to go and estimate the repairs . . .' Among the repairs were listed three damaged wheelbarrows!

The flowers of the holly are fragrant, and in May and June they can be found clustered in the leaf axils; indeed there seems no end to the attributes and advantages of the holly. Culpeper in 1643 claimed that it was governed by the planet Saturn and that it was good for the spleen, and the berries for colic, or as a purge. The Yerba Maté tea used in South America is made from holly bark, and it was the tea used by French, German and British troops as a stimulant during the First World War.

The holly tree enters much into folklore, and early Britons believed that the sun never deserted the tree and that it was therefore sacred; dwellings were decorated with holly, and other evergreens, so that woodland spirits might take refuge from the cold of winter. Beekeepers must not forget to put a sprig of holly on their hives to wish the bees a Happy Christmas – a very old English tradition.

At the foot of the holly hedge at Clarence House is a raised wooden platform on which the household staff stand to view Trooping the Colour, the arrival of heads of state, and other state processions, the most recent being the one for the wedding of the Duke and Duchess of York.

Above: Of course the corgis Ranger and Dash enjoy the garden too, sometimes at the expense of the more delicate herbaceous plants!

Opposite: The gardener, Terri-Janina Bijowska, has to sweep fallen twigs from around the base of the plane trees, taking care not to damage the spring bulbs.

This border has to suffer a fair battering during these occasions as staff, and sometimes corgis too, make their way across it to the wooden viewing platform. The other, rather different thing it suffers from is that seemingly eternal pest, bindweed (*Convolvulus major*); Bennie White used to derive great pleasure from following its roots relentlessly round the border, finally extracting them as best she might in great white lengths.

The steps at the west end of the raised walk are obscured by a large *Prunus serrulata purpurascens* 'Kanzan', and our way down them is blocked by its large trunk and branches, so we descend instead the steps by the little Lodge and once more find ourselves on the gravel path. Here we meet the present gardener, Terri-Janina Bijowska, who succeeded Bennie and whose first proper job was at Clarence House. Only twenty-two, Terri trained in the Royal Parks after a City and Guilds course in horticulture at Eltham, Middlesex, and began her garden work in Kensington Gardens and Hyde Park. She works single-handed except for occasional help to clear rubbish or hold a ladder, any lopping of trees being carried out by professional tree surgeons. She works from 7.30 a.m. until 4.00 p.m. and takes care not to wake Queen Elizabeth with any noisy jobs she may have to do, such as mowing the lawns. This takes one and a half days and is done once a week, or occasionally twice, usually on a Monday when the Queen Mother is least likely to be there. The gravel has to be raked once a week too, a back-breaking task.

The soil, a typical London acid one, has been thoroughly dug and fertilized over the years, a certain amount of horse manure from the Horse Guards being used and occasionally some peat, as in the hyacinth border. Terri has many ideas for improving the garden, with Her Majesty's preferences always borne in mind; she keeps her gardening books in the little Lodge used as a potting shed, where her tools also live, and refers frequently to them with an eagerness to learn more about the plants grown at Clarence House and about gardening in general.

Her main spring and summer work consists of the bedding and regular watering; this occasionally has to be done at weekends too, hoses only being used. The main work in the autumn and winter is the digging over and tidying of the beds and borders and the mulching and raking up of fallen leaves and twigs which, besides the fall from the trees in the garden, blow over in quantity from the Mall. Once gathered they are taken to Green Park, from where a contractor removes them.

On top of the great portico at Clarence House there are window-boxes; Terri has to plant these out and keep them watered, which she does precariously balanced on a ladder. In spring they are filled with yellow flowers – polyanthus and daffodils – in summer sometimes with geraniums, but more often with cinerarias. The flowers in the window-boxes, especially the polyanthus, are much molested by birds, but apart from the bindweed these are the only pests that are seriously troublesome in the Clarence House garden.

We now make our way to the east end of the garden, much of which is screened from our sight by various trees which we shall look at more closely in a moment. We pass along the gravel paths before the garden front of St James's Palace, and before we reach the path crossing the lawns from the little Lodge we notice several low ornamental trees growing on the lawn on our right. Two of them are *Malus floribunda rosea*, whose vivid pink flower-buds and blush pink flowers make a riot of blossom in the spring. There is a young *Magnolia grandiflora* 'Exmouth', planted by Queen Elizabeth, which has not yet flowered and which she feels should have done so by now as it has been in for a few years. Certainly this clone is one of the magnolias that normally does flower young, and this plant should soon be bearing its huge creamy-white flowers with their sweet smell of lemons. It is usually planted against a wall in this country, as is the large specimen on the terrace at Royal Lodge, but with the extra warmth of the London climate and the protection of a walled and sunny garden, it should also do well.

One of the good things about city gardens is that because of their sheltered nature and the warmth of the walls due to inside heating, a quite tender plant may survive where elsewhere it would certainly not be hardy (even olives ripen on an ancient tree in the Chelsea Physic Garden). The highest mean temperature

An *Acer palmatum* 'Senkaki', the beautiful coral-bark maple, has been planted by the Queen Mother at the east end of the garden.

in Great Britain is in central London, the weather being 3–4 degrees centigrade warmer than the average temperature elsewhere in the British Isles.

Also planted on this lawn are two weeping trees. These are *Caragana arborescens* 'Arbor Walker', brought by Queen Elizabeth from Royal Lodge for the garden here. The plant comes from Mongolia and Siberia and was introduced in 1752; it loves the sun, and its yellow pea flowers appear in May among foliage of a fresh and tender green. These particular plants are grafted on a straight stem, probably of the species, forming small weeping trees. Another small tree planted by Queen Elizabeth is the beautiful coral-bark maple, *Acer palmatum* 'Senkaki'. A native of Japan, it rarely grows taller than 20 feet; its young stems are coral red, and its leaves, so delicately cut, are bright clear green, turning in the autumn to a soft amber yellow. Growing not far from it is a considerably older tree, a single pink hawthorn.

Crossing the path from the little Lodge we find ourselves under the canopy of two fine lime trees, *Tilea europoea*, or *T. vulgaris* as it has more recently been called. The change of name in England from 'line' to 'lime' must have happened before 1684, between Shakespeare's time and John Evelyn's, because Evelyn in his *Sylva* of that date always writes of 'the lime tree or linden', while Shakespeare makes Ariel in *The Tempest* speak of 'the line grove'. The quality of the wood gave the tree its name, the root meaning of the word being 'smooth', and in Anglo-Saxon times it was used for making shields, to such an extent that 'lind' also meant a shield.

In later times the wood has been much used by carvers, and Evelyn tells us:

> Because of its colour and easy working, and that it is not subject to split, architects make of it models for their designed buildings; and the carvers in wood use it, not only for small figures, but for large statues and entire histories in bass and high reliefe; witness, beside several more, the festoons, fruitages, and other sculptures of admirable inventions, and performance to be seen about the choir of St Paul's and other churches, Royal Palaces, and noble houses in city and country; all of them the works and inventions of our Lysippus Mr [Grinling] Gibbons, comparable, and for ought appears equal, to anything of the antients. Having had the honour (or so I account it) to be the first to recommend this great artist to His Majesty Charles II, I mentione it on this occasion with much satisfaction.

Frequently planted in gardens, and often pleached or pruned for walks and arcades (in Le Nôtre's gardens forming great avenues), the lime, to quote Evelyn once more:

> . . . is most proper and beautiful for walks, as producing an upright Body, smooth and even Bark, ample Leaf, sweet Blossom, and goodly shade . . . is there a more ravishing or delightful object than to behold some entire streets and whole Towns planted with their Trees, in even lines before their doors, so as they seem like Cities in a wood? This is extremely fresh, and skreens the house both from the Winds, Sun and Dust; then which there can be nothing more desirable where streets are much frequented.

The scent of the lime is certainly one of summer's chief delights, pervading the air and attracting multitudes of bees. In their spreading glory, these two trees, which are probably more than 150 years old, cast their shade over the latest beds to be made in the Clarence House garden. They were dug and prepared under the limes in 1985, and planted with various shrubs. There is a *Camellia japonica elegans*; this is a free-flowering shrub with beautiful carmine flowers. The

Left: The lime, from John Evelyn's *Sylva* of 1662. The two spreading trees at Clarence House are probably more than 150 years old.
Right: Limewood is traditionally used for carving as it is exceptionally strong: a cravat of point-lace by Grinling Gibbons.

---

camellia genus was named by Linnaeus after George Kamel of Moravia, who had latinized his name to Camellus and wrote an account of plants on an island in the Philippines which he had visited – published in John Ray's *Historia Plantarum* of 1704. After the end of the Napoleonic War many hundreds of camellias were raised in Europe, first in England and later on the Continent, and they remained the most popular greenhouse plant nearly up to the close of the nineteenth century. Between the two world wars they had a renaissance as an outdoor shrub, hard winters having proved the camellia to be among the hardiest of all evergreens.

There are some azaleas growing here too – 'Brazil', a Knap Hill hybrid with bright tangerine-red flowers, with frilled edges that darken as they age, and 'Lapwing', as well as several plants of the fragrant *Rhododendron luteum* from

Left: A *Camellia japonica elegans* grows in the shadow of the lime trees.
Right: The luscious fruits of the black mulberry. The recently retired gardener, Bennie White, found they made an excellent pie, if she could get to them before the birds.

Asia Minor, the particular favourite of Queen Elizabeth's which is planted in such quantities at Royal Lodge. A group of *Hydrangea hortensis* is also here, and *Senecio greyii*, an evergreen shrub with white felted buds and undersides to its leaves that give it a silvered look – in contrast to its brilliant yellow daisy-like flowers. Two flowering currants, *Ribes sanguineum* 'King Edward VII', with their distinctive dry woody scent, another *Mahonia bealei* hybrid, some un-named heaths (as Queen Elizabeth pointed out, these were not flourishing as well as they might here), a *Hibiscus syriacus* and a bright flame-flowered chaenomeles make up the rest of the group. The soil in this large rambling bed under the shadow of the trees dries out very easily in the summer, and Terri has to do a great deal of watering as well as clearing up the leaves and flower bracts that seem to drop all through the year. A shaded garden is always difficult to maintain if a degree of colour is wanted, and this area is no exception to the rule; the sparrows using the dry soil as a dust bath in the warm months are perhaps happier than the plants!

Beyond the limes we come to the great mulberry tree planted in the time of James I, which we have already mentioned. Growing in the lawn, it leans like a tired old man over the path, but it still bears abundant fruit which Bennie White used, from time to time, to make into wine, or use in a pie.

Bennie tells how every year a pair of mallard made their nest under the mulberry, and when the young were hatched the mother duck would shepherd her brood to the gate by the Lodge; here she waited and quacked until Bennie arrived. She would then, with the help of two policemen, open the gates and, stopping the traffic in the Mall, personally escort the troupe to the pond in St James's Park where they happily launched themselves into the water!

This mulberry is the common or black mulberry (*Morus nigra*), a plant both architectural and picturesque. Its body is gnarled and rugged, its bare twigs make a thick 'knotted' tracery, and its foliage is luxuriant, composed of heart-shaped leaves, rough above and downy below, and forming a wide spreading head which in August is sprinkled with luscious and juicy fruit of a dark, almost black-red colour when fully ripe. Nearly an inch long, they are sweet to the taste, with an agreeable slightly sub-acid flavour, and make an excellent jelly.

Coming as they do from Western Asia, mulberries like a warm soil, well drained and loamy, and thrive exceedingly well in London, where James I planted the tree in great numbers. It spreads its fruits, the moment they are ripe, in a red-pink carpet in late summer beneath its canopy. For this reason the mulberry should always be planted on grass, or sheets should be spread beneath the trees so that the fruits can be picked up clean for eating and cooking. The mulberry will make an avenue of much dignity; if you should visit Selcuk in Turkey, or go to Lambay Island off Dublin Bay, you will be able to see two fine examples. The trees are very long-lived, but grow swiftly enough if they are thoroughly well planted and in a region congenial to them; quickly enough to give pleasure in one lifetime and a great deal of pleasure to posterity. We have much to thank King James for – seldom has so large a mistake had so rewarding an outcome.

There are several other interesting trees sharing this lawn with the mulberry: an ancient pear (*Pyrus communis*), which has long been cultivated in gardens, is thick with scented blossom in April, while its leaves, of a glossy green, sometimes turn the most beautiful colours in the autumn. Could this very tree be one of the fruit trees noticed by Sieur de Serre? It does look very old indeed. Beyond the pear is a living relic of the prehistoric age – a *Metasequoia glyptostroboides*, a tree first described by the botanist Miki from fossils he had discovered in Japan in the Lower Pliocene strata in 1941. The trees had grown in North America, Japan and Asia when these were all one land-mass. It is an extraordinary story, because in the very same year living specimens were found growing in China; a hundred trees were discovered in north-east Szechuan, happy among the oak and chestnut, in a wet soil and a mild winter temperature. Specimens were not collected until 1944, and seeds not until the autumn of 1947, when they were sent to the Arnold Arboretum, whence they were distributed in 1948 to many gardens in America and Europe. There is, sadly, no record in Europe of seed becoming fertile – the male cones do not ripen, as they seem to find the climate too cold and the growing season too short. The metasequoia is a tree of perfect symmetry, cone-shaped when young and growing rapidly, with leaves a bluish green above and light green below. In autumn they turn to rose and tawny amber, seeming as though caught in the rays of the rising sun.

Not far from the metasequoia is a very old crab-apple – a malus, but of what variety it is difficult to discover for it has been here a long time and its name has been lost in the mists of time. However, it is an exuberant tree, always covered in fruit, and Bennie White used to make the occasional pot of crab-apple jelly from it.

We now arrive at the broad border running under the east wall of the garden, and see in the southern end of the bed a large, oddly charming plant of rhubarb (*Rheum palmatum*). Its five-lobed leaves, large and spreading, are deeply cut, and the flowers, in a fluff of creamy yellow, shoot into the air on tall imposing stems. Behind the rhubarb, and growing on the west-facing wall, is a large *Wisteria sinensis*, the 'Chinese wisteria'. Not in flower until May, it is then one of the finest sights imaginable, but to look really well it must be ruthlessly pruned and grown in the sun. Queen Elizabeth has several other specimens too, at Royal Lodge. The Portuguese, who grow it wonderfully, say we do not prune it hard enough in this country and should cut it back mercilessly in the winter and again, but more lightly, in August. This harsh treatment will encourage more abundant flowering, and hard work will bring a delightful reward.

When wisteria was first grown in England in the early nineteenth century, it was thought that it would need to be grown in heat, but people soon realized that if it were to flower well all it needed was a sunny place, good loamy soil and some hard pruning. It will grow 100 feet, leaping up through tall trees, its trunk sometimes as thick as 5 feet and its flowers falling in showers of melting lavender in May. Trained over the hedge in Claude Monet's garden at Giverny, it hangs, its flowers deliciously scented, over the famous lake of water-lilies.

Next to the wisteria on the west-facing wall is an old lilac (*Syringa sinensis*) of unknown variety, and beyond, again, scrambling freely with a mass of stems and waving sprays rising above the wall, is a Banksian rose (*Rosa banksia* 'Lutea'), the 'Yellow Banksia', a rose with umbels of lightly scented, pale butter-yellow flowers borne in May. Queen Elizabeth finds it does not flower very well in the garden here, perhaps because of the large trees at this end of the garden which cut it off from the rays of the western sun. It is more successful at Royal Lodge where, as we have seen, it is also grown near wisteria.

Opposite: The glowing autumn colour of *Metasequoia glyptostroboides*. There is a young specimen of this fascinating prehistoric tree on the lawn by the mulberry.

We turn to our left now and arrive in the south-west corner of the garden to find a small collection of sculptures embraced by the leaves and yellow flowers, some self-sown, of _Hypericum petulatum_ var. _forrestii_, a free-seeding plant which has settled itself here and there along the foot of the palace wall. It is accompanied by one or two plants of _Acanthus mollis_; introduced into this country from southern Europe in the sixteenth century, this is almost ineradicable and could well have been here since that date. Its foliage was used in classical times, and is still used today, as a model for architectural decoration. Wreathed by the hypericum is a terracotta urn, and beside it is an unfinished head of an Indian woman, carved from a piece of stone brought back from Canada, and a touching statue of a small dachshund called 'Hanni' by Helena Gleichen, dated 1897–1912.

Walking back to the house along the gravel, past the bare, handsome walls of St James's Palace (free of climbers for security reasons) on your right, and the plane trees with the park beyond to your left, you are struck by the extraordinary calm of the garden. As you stop to admire a sundial by the great portico and smell again that bed of hyacinths or heliotrope, you wonder how this calm has been achieved in the heart of London. Is it simply the stately trees and smooth lawns which are the garden's main features, or does it also come from the idiosyncratic blend of formal and informal, and the elegant and cheerful planting? However that may be, we do feel that the gardens at Clarence House must surely provide for the Queen Mother the pleasure and relief described by the anonymous author of the 'Letter to Christopher Wren':

> _Fountains and Trees our wearied Pride_
> _Do please_
> _Even in the midst of Gilded Palaces_
> _And in our towns, that Prospect gives_
> _Delight_
> _Which opens round the country to our sight._

Opposite: Rosa banksia 'Lutea' scrambles freely over the west-facing wall. A favourite of the late King, it is also grown at Royal Lodge where it usually flowers more successfully, perhaps because here it is partly shaded by neighbouring trees.

Castle of Mey

CAITHNESS

The Castle of Mey is a hidden castle, hidden in the billowing woods which are so unexpectedly met as you arrive by the narrow, winding road from Wick. Not one tree has been seen on the way, and suddenly here is a little forest of them, their tops sculpted and shaped by the hand of the wind which has blown ceaselessly throughout the centuries.

A visitor gets an intimation of the remote spirit of the place with the first sight of the castle. A cluster of towers rises above the woods which embower it – the sea, blue and brilliant, stretches from the trees to a shadow on the far horizon which is Orkney and the Old Man of Hoy. This is the land of Caithness, the remotest peninsula on the mainland of Great Britain, over 800 miles from Cornwall's Land's End. It is a romantic land, made so by the hand of man as well as by that of nature. Ancient sites are scattered over it, monuments left by Stone Age man, like the Grey Cairns of Camster, built by people who worshipped an earth goddess and where, over 4,500 years ago, they buried their chiefs. These Stone Age people were the first settled farmers to arrive in Britain; later, the Bronze Age people left their mark with the great fan-shaped rows of standing stones on the southern slope of a low hill known as the 'Hill of Many Stanes'. After the Bronze Age a veil encompasses this distant land and its history, and we can only guess at the character and traditions of the people who lived there until the arrival of the Christians. Legend holds that St Columba brought the Faith to Caithness while St Ninian, who had been consecrated a bishop in Rome and was one of the first of the great Christian missionaries to

---

Opposite: Sycamores, their trunks bent into weird shapes by the wind, lend a fairytale atmosphere to the castle approach.

Left: Caithness abounds in prehistoric remains such as these standing stones at Stenness on Orkney. A watercolour by James Cassie.
Right: The romantic ruins of fifteenth-century Giringoe Castle, once the seat of the Earls of Caithness.

Alban, sent disciples north to convert the people. These missionaries made their way up the Great Glen from Solway, reaching Sutherland and Caithness in about 398 A D, and later penetrated further still to Shetland and the Orkneys. As we look across the wild waters of the Pentland Firth we can see the Isles of Orkney lying like stranded whales upon the northern horizon, and we admire and wonder at the courage of these Christians taking their frail craft across the treacherous seas, and of their faith in the power of Christ to take them to safety.

Ancient castles abound in Caithness, looking almost impossibly romantic and impregnable on the clifftops, protected from attack on either side by the deep inlets of the sea. The first castle builders up here were the Viking chiefs or 'jarls', and some of the castles still stand as reminders of the time Vikings held sway here, though most are now ruins, used only as landmarks for ships.

From the end of the eighth century the Norsemen began to gain a foothold on the islands and coasts of northern Scotland, and 100 years later they had conquered Caithness and Sutherland. Led by notorious pirates and freebooters, such as Sweyn Asliefsson, they ranged as far as Ireland, Cornwall and the Isle of Man, pillaging, plundering and harrying, returning to feast in their strongholds in Caithness. The grim and inaccessible ruin of Bucholie Castle was once

106

Lambaborg, the stronghold of the infamous Sweyn; Oldwick Castle or 'The Old Man of Wick' was once used for the flaunting and glittering feasts of Viking noblemen. Now it stands roofless and gaunt, but still three storeys high and with walls more than 8 feet thick.

For many centuries Caithness was so far removed from the centre of power in Scotland that the Vikings continued to rule, settling and mingling with the local inhabitants and making the fertile north-east of the country the foodstore for their empire. They bequeathed their place-names to many of the towns and villages, hamlets and farms – names such as Freswick and Lybster, Keiss and Scrabster. It is known that the Norse governors of Caithness lived hereabouts, and some people think that a recently discovered Viking house near John o'Groats may have been their official residence. The pirate Sweyn was the Governor's son, and the story goes that as a child he was out with his mother when his father's enemies struck, attacking the Governor's house and burning him alive within it. Sweyn swore vengeance, and when he reached manhood he put the descendants of the murderers to the sword, burning their homes to the ground.

There are other castles still to be seen of the twenty-eight known to have existed in this violent land: Giringoe and Sinclair, built on the coast north of Wick in the fifteenth and seventeenth centuries respectively. Giringoe was a seat of the Earls of Caithness, and Sinclair features in the dark stories handed down from the days of Earl George, who imprisoned his son for six years in the dungeons of his fortress. The young 'Master of Caithness' died in torment, having been fed only with salt meat and been forbidden water on the orders of his father.

Violent though the history of the area is, the land itself is more placid; you will find no rugged mountains here, indeed the difference from the Highlands is striking. The wide vistas of the Pentland Firth reveal sweeping heather-covered moor, patched with black bog, where the cotton grass shows white like fluffs of wool against the sable background, and vivid grass and gorse in glistening bloom stand out in contrast to the bog. The hills are gentle and rolling, the pastureland lush, and the wild moorland is broken by lochs and rivers where anglers such as Queen Elizabeth can find the wild brown trout, the sea trout and the salmon, which bend the rod with fighting vigour and whose flesh is pink and sweet to the taste. Out at sea, beyond the spectacular coastline, with its fishing harbours, soaring cliffs, rocky coves, and vast empty beaches, you can catch the giant halibut. The waters run clean off the Caithness coast, and sole and wrasse, cod and ling, brill and mackerel (fish names sounding like a carillon of bells) sweep in to feed on the fresh plankton brought in each day by the labyrinthine currents. Trawlers do not come here because of these tumultuous currents and because the sea bed is rocky and uneven, so it is the fisherman with

Left: The area around Mey provides wonderfully varied fishing for enthusiasts such as
Queen Elizabeth. *Salmon and Trout on a River Bank* by Victorian artist John Russell.
Right: Birds and wild flowers add to the enchantment of the Wick coast and moorlands.
Peter Graham, *A Nesting Place – Gannets.*

the rod who reigns supreme, while the golden eagles and the kestrel rule the
sky. You may see the stately gannet falling from the blue like a bolt to pierce
with its lethal beak the fish it has marked in the waters below; and on the high,
fissured sandstone cliffs puffins, kittiwakes, shags and guillemots have their
nests.

The fisherman can cast his fly too into many a fine river – the Thurso (a river
Her Majesty The Queen Mother regularly fishes) and the Wick, Berriedale and
Wester Water – landing trout and silver salmon on moor or in glen, or walking
through the heather to reach some of Caithness's hundred shallow lochs. Their
waters are only 5 or 6 feet deep and are scattered over a land left to the nibbling

sheep, the red deer and the fox. Here in the far north land the light lasts long in the summer days and you may wander late over the great moorlands and pastures, perhaps discovering as you go the precious wild flowers that are found only in Caithness, Sutherland and Orkney: the Scottish primrose (*Primula scotica*) with its clustered pink and purple flowers, the frog and heath spotted orchids, the Baltic rush, or, at Reay, *Euphrasia brevipila* sp. *reayensis*, an eyebright which grows only in this one place. Birch and bird cherry, aspen and juniper clothe the rocky gorges through which rivers tumble; and growing beneath them are the burnet rose, bugle and ramsons, woodruff and willow.

It was only with the extraordinary boom in the fishing industry in the early years of the nineteenth century that Caithness emerged from the mists that had wrapped it for centuries. 'Silver darlings' the Caithness people called the herring, for it was to them that they owed the improvement in their livelihood. The numerous small harbours tucked between high cliffs or looking over sandy beaches were built then, and with the building of the railways lobsters and crabs could be sent in great quantities to the markets in the south. Before the nineteenth century there was no proper road to Caithness, and its trade links were all by sea to the ports of north-west Europe – which traders used rather than those in Great Britain. It is a strange thought that Caithness is nearer to the Arctic circle than it is to London, and that the nearest seat of government lies in the Faroe Islands. In recent years oil has been discovered off her coasts and an atomic station has been built at Dounreay; many thousands of people now find work there. Under the shallow waters of the Moray Firth lie vast quantities of coal and, in the greatest bogs in the kingdom, lie millions of tons of peat. So this countryside, for long shrouded in mystery, has come into the light of the twentieth century, though still retaining much of its extraordinary romance.

This then is the land that surrounds the Castle of Mey and its garden which I have come to see. To know something of the country, its aspect and character, as well as a little of its history, will I hope set the scene and help us to understand the atmosphere and indefinable charm of the garden. For charm it most surely possesses, and this is, I suggest, as much due to its attachment to a historic house and a countryside whose appearance and vegetation has been shaped and conditioned by the climate and by events as it is to the taste and affection for certain plants and flowers of its owner, Queen Elizabeth The Queen Mother, whose home it has been for over thirty years.

When I drove from Wick on my first visit, the sun was shining from a sky of clear blue reflected in the seas and all around was a sense of immense space and light, created by the wide horizons and the low gently rolling country with almost nothing perpendicular to arrest the eye. Even the cottages were mostly one-storeyed; some were abandoned crofts with roofs open to the air, others had slate roofs, castellated gable ends and a few scattered shrubs, wallflowers and clumps of narcissi growing in their gardens, alongside the solid leaves of rhubarb. Sheep and cows grazed the brilliant green fields, their boundaries marked by large stone slabs propped edge-to-edge like rows of gravestones; while here and there gorse and buttercups studded the pastures with flashes of gold. From a stretch of sooty bog a curlew, that sentinel-in-chief of the wastes, rose with slow, measured wing-beats and gave its cry of 'cour lieu', but I looked in vain for the golden eagle I knew to be at home here.

The road turned and twisted, sometimes obscuring and sometimes revealing the rough, irregular coastline, while white surf broke on the beaches and seabirds rose from the black cliffs. The car passed Canisbay Kirk – a modest medieval building, whose pillared and be-urned tombs are in extravagant contrast to its simplicity. It is here that the Queen Mother comes to worship when she is at the Castle of Mey. As I drew nearer, the castle began to emerge from the trees – when the Queen Mother is at home her personal standard is clearly visible, flaunting gaily from its staff, tugged by the fierce wind. Some modern bungalows are passed ('Royal Crescent') and a filling station ('Castle View'), reminding us that we are firmly in the twentieth century.

The entrance to the drive is marked by stone pillars, surrounded by stunted trees of sycamore and ash, thorn, chestnut and hazel and a few firs; along either side of the gateway is a clipped beech hedge. The curving drive passes between dense hedges, a tapestry of thorn, rowan and copper beech made even thicker, I subsequently discovered, with cuttings taken by the gardener at the castle. The hedges stand back from the drive, separated from it by a wide band of long grass sprinkled with wild flowers: daisies and buttercups, a mist of Queen Anne's lace and lady's smock, while fronds of ferns spring from the foot of the hedge. After a few hundred yards a low hexagonal lodge comes into view, peering from a heavy shelter of sycamores, the green door and pointed windows, diamond-paned, giving it a touch of mock Gothic romanticism. Passing through this second gateway with its robust pillars of square stone, its gates of heavy trellised wood flung back, I drive under the thick canopy of sycamore trees, their arching branches echoing the shape of the lodge windows. To the left a high wall rises, perhaps 10 feet or more, and beneath the trees on either side there are walks mown through grass that is thick with more wild flowers. By May the daffodils are faded, but London Pride dusts the lush green with its pale rose flowers and there is a wave of bluebells under some newly-planted ash trees. Aberdeen Angus cattle, black as night, graze with their calves in the meadow beyond the trees. Then all at once, rounding a left-hand curve in the drive, I am confronted by the castle.

It does not look as one's fancy might picture a castle in this remote part of Great Britain: grey-stoned, small-windowed, perhaps somewhat forbidding,

The castle sits in a hollow, protected from the wind by high stone walls and on three sides by a mantle of woodland.

---

under a lowering sky. No, this castle is bonny and gay, with large white-painted windows set in rosy-coloured stone. On this particular day the towers are silhouetted against a brilliant blue sky (not that this was such a rare occurrence, as I was to learn later). There is too an atmosphere of smiling welcome about the place, encouraged by the warm colour of the sandstone, the sparkling windows and the daisy-studded lawns about its walls.

The castle sits in a hollow as though seeking shelter from the storms, the woods gathered like a protecting shawl about its southern side. The trees – sycamores, one of the toughest of all trees – lean to the east, their tops swept aside by the continual north-west wind. In their shadows, beneath their lichened boles patched in silver and charcoal, a golden carpet of celandines is spread, and later bluebells and fair maids of France (*Ranunculus aconitifolius* 'Flore Pleno') appear. The leaves of the ranunculus are strong and deeply cut, a dark almost black green, and above them float exquisite double buttons of purest white.

Only yards below the castle on the eastern side are the sea and the rocky shore, and to the south the land slopes away over the grasslands of the Royal Farm, cattle and sheep dotting the orderly patterns of fields whose squares and rectangles contrast with the chasmal beauty of the shore. On the spring day of my first visit, the opal and sapphire of the sea reflected the intense blue of the sky, its surface shadows continually changed by the clouds chasing across the void.

> *Like a painted map the landscape lies;*
> *And wild above shine the cloud-thronged skies*
> *That chase each other on with hurried pace*
> *Like living things as if they ran a race.*
> *The winds that o'er each sudden tempest brood*
> *Waken like spirits in a startled mood*
> *Flirting the sear leaves on the bleaching lea . . .*

JOHN CLARE

In its remoteness and isolation the castle might have seemed a lonely place, but I had no sense of this; I was conscious only of a pleasant spirit of mysterious solitude, but at the same time a lively one. The strong towers, the views along the curving bay and over the sea to Orkney, and the sunny pastureland under the open skies of the changing seasons, give the Castle of Mey far too happy an aspect for it to seem lonely. But a royal castle set in so romantic a situation, hidden in woods at the brink of the ocean, stirs the imagination to all kinds of fancies about its past history and inhabitants. However, I found that in reality these had been less violent and dramatic than elsewhere in Caithness, such as at Sinclair Castle. Mey was built in the sixteenth century, between 1566 and 1572, by George, 4th Earl of Caithness, whose second son George inherited on the early death of his elder brother. George founded the baronetical family of Sinclair of Mey, but the older Sinclair line became extinct in 1789 and the Mey family succeeded to the earldom; for the next 100 years the Castle of Mey became its family seat.

It has been said that the castle was used as a grain store by the Norsemen. It is a typical keep of the sixteenth century, built to a 'Z' plan with vaulting on the ground floor and above the main staircase; its great hall is 40 feet in length and its masonry walls are 6 feet thick, with numerous gun-holes in the ground and first

A view from the lawn at the Castle of Mey. Although the garden may be in one of the most northern settings of the British Isles, it is also in one of the most beautiful.

floors, and although additions to the castle have been made over the years, these are discreet and modest and have not spoiled its character.

The story of how the Castle of Mey became the Queen Mother's home is well known. Found and chosen by her and therefore unique among her four houses, she bought it in 1952, soon after the death of the King. The mourning Queen had been staying quietly with her old friends, Commander and Lady Doris Vyner, at the 'House of the Northern Gate', when they mentioned to her that Old Barrogill Castle – as Mey was once called – was for sale.

Queen Elizabeth paid several visits to the castle, its surrounding twenty-five acres of land and its walled garden, each time more attracted by the idea of making it hers. It was by this time in a fairly ruinous condition, and the owner, Captain Imbert-Terry, who had left the place after his wife's death, had considered pulling it down. Queen Elizabeth says that it was largely because of this threat to destroy it that her decision to buy was made: it was one of the few castles left in this area, besides being quite a historic one, and she felt she could not let it be pulled down.

The Queen Mother loves the hugeness of the open spaces and the sense of restfulness the singularities of the Caithness landscapes give. In spite of the unceasing wind and wild weather, Her Majesty finds a feeling of peace and freedom in this countryside to which she has grown deeply attached. Queen Elizabeth makes several visits to her home during the year: when the silver salmon are running in the river Thurso, for she is a keen and skilled fisher-woman, in the month of August when she has friends to stay, and in early October, when autumn's breath is on the air.

> *Down from the branches fall the leaves,*
> *A waness comes on all the trees,*
> *The summer's done,*
> *And into his last house in Heaven*
> *Now goes the Sun.*

> (Medieval Latin Lyric)

It is for these visits, at the summer's end and at the autumn's beginning, when she comes to manage the estate, that the gardener, Mr Sandy Webster, works throughout the year, so as to have everything at its very best for the Queen Mother's coming. This is the nineteenth year that Mr Webster has been at the Castle of Mey; he came from Birkhall in 1967, where he worked under his brother. (He remembers that it then took them six weeks to rake the leaves and turn them into a 15-foot-high compost heap!) His aim has been to make the

---

Opposite: Mr Webster shows the author around the garden. He has nineteen years' experience of the castle's unique problems.

Above: Stone walls, 15 feet high, surround the gardens. Without them most plants would be burned by the ceaseless north-west wind.

Opposite: The rosy stone and large windows make this more welcoming and comfortable than most Scottish castles. The wind may be merciless in winter, but the sun shines often during the Queen Mother's visits.

castle garden perfect for the Queen Mother's visits, just as his wife (the castle housekeeper) strives unfailingly to make the light and pretty rooms welcoming and comfortable.

His great enemy is the wind, which can reach ninety miles per hour, and his battles against its depredations are joined in every quarter of the garden, not least in the walled garden lying to the west of the castle. In spite of the height of its rosy-coloured granite walls (10 feet high – and 15 feet on the north-west) the racing air surges over their tops, battering and burning the plants within, sometimes turning them quite black in a matter of minutes, and at other times completely flattening them. Mr Webster has even seen cabbages hurled over the highest part of the wall by the wind, and though the degrees of frost rarely exceed 5 or 6, the trees will only grow to the height of the wall. None the less, a great many plants do grow within and without these walls, and Queen Elizabeth The Queen Mother has triumphantly succeeded in creating a garden

bursting with flowers and shrubs, vegetables and fruit. It has a delightful air about it of old-fashioned homeliness and abundance, and at the same time it produces, as so many old-fashioned gardens do, all that is needed for the house. Within its walls I met the sous-chef, in checked trousers, white apron and knotted kerchief, carrying a large bowl to collect redcurrants for the kitchen, and a footman picking flowers from one of the borders, to be arranged in the dining-room and drawing-room and other rooms in the castle. The vases will be packed with all the simple cottage flowers – antirrhinums and marigolds, godetias, roses and daisies. The homely mixture, so loved by the Queen Mother, of fruit, vegetables and flowers reminds me of what was to George Eliot, too, the ideal garden:

> A charming paradisiacal mingling of all that was pleasant to the eyes and good for food . . . you gathered a Moss Rose one moment and a bunch of currants the next; you were in a delicious fluctuation between the scent of Jasmine and the juice of Gooseberries; the crimson of a Carnation was carried out in the lurking of the neighbouring Strawberry Beds.

Here, then, there is both beauty and utility, each complementing and enhancing the other, with a seemingly careless and yet thoughtful fusion of colour and design created by practical necessity and personal taste.

But let us now return to our exploration of the garden. On the left and right are rows of the huge stone flags that we saw dividing the fields on our drive from Wick. At Mey they form an enclosure for the entrance front, running in front of the trees which cluster on either side. The slabs on the right hand are heightened by a rustic-poled trellis, which the Queen Mother says was put there as a windbreak. There is a castellated low stone wall surmounted by cannons, moved from the ruined coastal battery which can be seen from the castle. They were intended 'for use against Napoleon', Her Majesty points out, 'and in the last war there was a fighter squadron stationed up here to fight Hitler'.

Above: The Queen Mother enjoys growing vegetables as well as flowers, and has this delightful pair of eighteenth-century Chelsea pea-pods in her china collection.
Opposite: The Queen Mother and the author enjoy a stroll in the garden at Mey. Her Majesty has created an abundant cottage garden in one of the most remote and inhospitable parts of the British Isles.

Nearby, two ash trees (one of which has since been replaced) were planted in 1875 by the then Prince and Princess of Wales, and a wise choice they were, for no tree can compare with the ash for strength and anchorage against the gale, its tough roots winding themselves into the crevices of rocks and ranging to astonishing distances. It is a tree held in high honour by the Scots, in the past furnishing the staves for their national weapon, the pike. It was a handful of Scots under Moray, brandishing pike-shafts, who repulsed de Clifford's cavalry in 1314 and supported Edward Bruce at Bannockburn, enabling him to hurl the English army into confusion among the Milton bogs, thus setting the seal on Scottish independence.

I return now to the peaceful scene laid out on the southern side of the castle. Beyond the cannons, daisy-sprinkled grass forms an oval of green before the entrance, and wooden tubs on either side of the front door are filled in late summer with pink petunias, collarette dahlias and nasturtiums. A castellated high wall runs east from the castle, the path at its foot leading to a wicket gate. All is shadowed and quiet here, and the path through the gate is paved with irregular stone; a wide border on the left planted with various shrubs has been overcome by bishop's weed and is due to be replanted. It will be a hard task to eliminate this pest; even the tiniest piece of root left in the ground will start it off again and in no time at all the beastly bishop will be back in force, swamping precious plants in nauseous green waves. This bane of all gardeners used not to be so universally disliked. It was introduced by monks in the Middle Ages as a cure for gout, and was given its common name later because it was so often found growing near ecclesiastical ruins. The great botanist Linnaeus did not share our distaste for it either, growing it especially to eat as salad.

There are some newly planted species roses on the right of this path which seem to be flourishing, and behind them are the trees of the wood, the sycamores, throwing their shade over the path and border, their branches and trunks looking, in their twists and contortions, like trees in an Arthur Rackham painting. Queen Elizabeth thinks they must be about 150 years old and wonders at the good fortune of having a wood in such a place. In the spring the sadness of the wood is bright with young green sprays; there are no bluebells, but snowberry and the fair maids of France grow, and a clearing, where once a conservatory stood, is lit in the month of August with the pale yellow scented flowers of *Primula florindae*.

To the west of the castle another high wall links the house to the enclosed garden, broken only by a wide gateway whose solid stone piers frame a pathway that leads to the Royal Farm and the sea, a short step away over the silvery turf. For a moment it does not seem too fanciful to imagine a ship riding at anchor in the gusting wind, waiting for some shadowy figure – a Norseman perhaps – to embark.

A mass of heavily-scented *Primula florindae* fills a clearing in the wood where once a conservatory stood.

There is a border at the foot of this wall, filled in late summer with massed ranks of bedding plants – dark blue lobelia, single-flowered dahlias, antirrhinums in mixed colours, sweet white alyssum and begonias threaded from end to end of the border like a thick pink ribbon. The wall has ten plants of the rambler rose 'Albertine' planted along its length, their coppery-pink flowers and deeper salmon-red buds, strongly scented of apples, so thickly massed that the shiny foliage can scarcely be seen. 'Albertine' is a cross of 1931 between *Rosa wichuriana* and a rose called 'Mrs Arthur Robert Waddell'; it stands up strongly

to bad weather, flowering at Mey many weeks later than it would in the south and having a much longer flowering season than the warmth of the south allows. To the Queen Mother she is 'dear old Albertine, ready to stand anything'. Hung in delicate curtains of yellow among the roses is the canary creeper (*Tropaeoleum peregrinum*), and in the border among the bedding is a large bush of forsythia (*Forsythia* × *intermedia* 'Spectabilis') which comes out here in the late spring, its golden flowers wreathing the branches before the leaves appear.

The outer side of the wall of the enclosed garden, facing east, has more 'Albertine' and more canary creeper, with a clematis hybrid scrambling among them. The border at its foot is planted thickly with the hybrid tea rose 'Silver Jubilee' and some plants of 'Iceberg', a floribunda rose raised by Kordes in Germany in 1958 and then called 'Schneewittchen'. This famous rose, with its bunches of white semi-double flowers, is supposed to be tough and hardy, but it does not look very happy here. Perhaps the wind at Mey is too much for even its constitution, although in general this hybrid does appear to have lost some of its original vigour. Dividing this border is a raised stone platform supporting two green-painted seats; tubs on either side of them are filled in late summer with nasturtiums, flowers loved with nostalgia by Queen Elizabeth, whose childhood garden they remind her of, and where 'they shared a place with radishes and one rose'.

Above: The simple nasturtium, held in great affection by the Queen Mother because it reminds her of her childhood, is grown in several places in the garden.
Opposite: The coppery-pink flowers of 'dear old Albertine, ready to stand anything'.

123

A solid wooden gate set in the wall leads into the enclosed garden, a typical two-and-a-half-acre Scottish castle kitchen garden, dating from the eighteenth century when self-sufficiency was essential. It is one of the few survivors of these gardens (for as a result of excessively high labour costs, nearly all the kitchen gardens in Scotland had disappeared by 1960); another example not far away is a hidden garden with walls of lovely old stone at the House of Tongue, the home of the Countess of Sutherland. Here, too, the garden is divided into compartments, surrounded by thick hedges where fruit, flowers and vegetables are grown all together.

The Queen Mother loves this manner of growing plants, not only for its practicality (for the garden here must and does supply all the castle's needs) but also for the beauty that the intermingling of the various fruits, flowers and vegetables brings to the scene. It is, too, another nostalgic reminder of the homes of her childhood, where the plantings were similarly planned.

The first defence against the wind in this walled garden is a grid of thick, clipped hedges; like the hedges along the drive they are 'tapestry hedges', that is to say they are made up of a dense mixture of elder (some of which is a

Thick tapestry hedges divide the garden into 'rooms' and give vital protection from the wind. They also make it an exciting, secretive place to visit.

variegated form), *Rosa rugosa*, berberis, copper beech, fuchsia, laburnum, hawthorn, honeysuckle and privet, with patches of currant, their leaves strongly scenting the air, sown here and there by the birds. They provide a rich back-drop in varied green – a 'verdure' tapestry – for the flowers and vegetables as well as protection from the elements. At the same time, they give a sense of secrecy and mystery to the garden by dividing it into a series of sheltered 'rooms' – you do not know what plantings or designs you will find until you have rounded the corner of the next hedge.

It is to this garden, with its hedged and hidden parts, planted thick with vegetables and burgeoning flowers, that Queen Elizabeth The Queen Mother comes, sometimes more than once in the day. She comes to walk her dogs, the young corgis Ranger and Dash, and to enjoy her plants: the old hybrid perpetual rose with its Tyrian purple flowers and heady scent, which surely must have grown for nearly a century on this same spot, and her beloved sweet peas, scrambling in a confusion of washed pinks, blues and mauves up a tall barrier, its spruce branches and wires now quite hidden by the peas' thick growth.

> *Here are sweetpeas, on tip-toe for a flight,*
> *With wings of gentle flush o'er delicate white*
> *And taper fingers catching at all things*
> *To bind them all about with tiny rings.*
>
> JOHN KEATS

In spite of the high walls and hedges, Queen Elizabeth finds that the wild weather – not so much the cold (after all the Gulf Stream washes the waters round the coast), but the ceaseless wind – makes the garden at Mey very unpredictable. Not many plants will stand up to the gales, but the gardener must discover which ones will and stick to them. It is the uncertainty of what is going to survive the winds and winters that makes the choice of plants a difficult one, coupled with the fact that they must be capable of flowering during the weeks that the Queen Mother is at Mey. Everything is timed to be ready for these visits, and because the climate delays flowering times by at least a month, this is not very difficult to achieve. However, Her Majesty is never certain what she will be able to count on, and in the early days of her gardening here she tried a large number of different plants, many of which did not succeed. The climate of the garden is capricious, a fighting challenge to any gardener. After all, it is one of the most northern in the British Isles, and the surrounding countryside does suggest that little but grass and heather should survive.

With a first glimpse of the walled garden, it is realized how successfully Queen Elizabeth The Queen Mother has managed to outwit the wind, through choosing to grow only plants and flowers that have proved themselves, over the

The hardy agapanthus 'Headbourne Worthy' hybrids have proved themselves well able to resist the winds.

years, able to resist it. The hardy agapanthus 'Headbourne Worthy' hybrids, with umbels of flowers in varying shades of blue, are a group of plants that have proved themselves, in spite of having been raised from crosses of species collected in South Africa. The shrubby potentillas also flourish, and there are several good hybrids of *P. fruticosa* with abundant flowers of creamy white, primrose and deep yellow; I noticed 'Katherine Dykes' as well as 'Elizabeth', 'Telford Cream', 'Moonlight', and 'Tangerine' with its dusty orange flowers. The new hybrid 'Princess', which has beautiful blush-pink flowers, was still in its pot awaiting planting when I visited.

The blue and silver flower-heads of eryngium, looking as though they are cut from some delicate metal.

Huge bushes of *Fuchsia magellanica* grow on either side of the gates as you enter and give immediate shelter, their flowers like little scarlet flames against the deep green leaves; these 'hedges' are backed by a wall of huge stone slabs standing upright edge-to-edge against the hedge which rises high above them. These slabs are used in this manner throughout the garden and are an unusual feature of it. Turning to the right, there is a broad border under the west-facing wall which is closely planted with a mixture of herbaceous plants and small shrubs; besides the potentillas there is a large clump of *Chrysanthemum maxima* 'Everest' with golden-centred daisy flowers, a *Spiraea bumalda* with flat reddish

Left: Shrubby potentillas such as the hybrid 'Telford Cream' seem to flourish.
Right: Anemone hupehensis was found growing in a Chinese cemetery by Robert Fortune
in the nineteenth century.

flowers on a 3-foot bush, which is in flower continuously, *Lysimachia punctata* with bright yellow flowers in whorls on its 2-foot erect stems, and an eryngium, un-named but possibly *E. alpinum* 'Donald', its blue and silver flower-heads looking as though cut from some delicate metal. A pink *Anemone hupehensis* is in flower; this plant was discovered by Robert Fortune, who had been sent to China in 1842 by the Far East Committee of the Royal Horticultural Society. He arrived in Shanghai on the day the post was officially opened for trade by the British Council, and first noticed the anemone growing in a Chinese cemetery. Specimens were sent back to England in the revolutionary portable closed greenhouse, invented in 1829 by a London doctor, Nathaniel Ward, and known as a 'Wardian Case', in which plants could live for several years if necessary and thus survive the journey home.

Growing not far from the anemone is that beauty, *Campanula lactiflora* 'Loddon Anna', with its pale mushroom-pink flowers, and *Geranium* 'A. T. Johnson', as well as the spectacular *G. psilostemon* with magenta dark-centred flowers, and the double violet-blue *G. ibericum*; all seem happy here. Mixed petunias are planted here and there in the front of the border, and there is a narrow band of mown grass on either side of the gravel path edging the borders or beds. The long 4-foot-wide bed to the left is filled with astilbe (*A.* × *arendsii*) in deep and pale pinks, with a hedge forming part of the 'grid' system behind it. The planting everywhere is close; in this way Queen Elizabeth feels the plants give each other shelter and support.

Abundant colour bursts forth in each of the quadrangles. The planting everywhere is close; in this way Queen Elizabeth feels the plants give each other shelter and support.

The path turns to the left, and running in a thick band of shaded yellow, their scent heavy on the air, is a mass of *Primula florindae*, again backed by one of the 'tapestry' hedges. To the right rises an even higher wall, facing south, and with a very deep border in front of it. Against the wall, and heavily clothing it, are huge plants of *Buddleia davidii*, a large *Fuchsia riccartonii* and an escallonia (*E. macrantha*) with pink flowers and shiny dark green leaves.

The Queen Mother finds that the primula seeds itself everywhere, and also finds that the buddleias do well and bring the bees. There is one outstanding beauty among them, with pale fat pinkish-lavender flowers, shorter than the racemes of the common buddleias and without the plant's usual tiresome habit of dying at the end; this buddleia came from Lord Stairs's garden at Lochinch and is probably an especially good form of the plant of that name, now in commerce. *Buddleia davidii*'s common name is 'butterfly bush', and well named it is, for when it is in flower its long scented racemes of purple, white or lavender do indeed seem particularly attractive to butterflies. The plant was discovered by Abbé David in China as recently as 1869, Farrer and William Purdom bringing back specimens to this country, but it quickly became very popular and has naturalized itself in many waste places, especially on old bomb sites in London, since the last war.

Like the buddleia, a gigantic bush of the evergreen shrub *Senecio greyii*, with its silver-margined grey leaves and daisy-like deep yellow flowers, is left unpruned so as to give extra protection from the wind. Also on this great wall are fruit trees – two apples, espaliered and ancient, their lichen-covered branches knotted and gnarled. In their shelter grow roses – hybrid teas and floribundas, whose names have been lost – some mauve hybrids of *Phlox paniculata*, and a soft pink *Achillea millefolium* – petunias and pansies fill any bare spaces. Queen Elizabeth loves violas and pansies, and there is a charming blue-mauve variety of which Her Majesty is particularly fond, showing bright flowers above the green and silver leaves of *Lamium maculatum*. The pansy is one of the few flowers which has not lost favour with gardeners through many centuries, or been subject to capricious affections influenced by the fashions of the age. We remember too the late King's love for these flowers and how he made a pansy garden at Balmoral.

> *I pray what flowers are these?*
> *The pansy this;*
> *O, that's for lovers' thoughts*
>
> BEN JONSON

Opposite: Bouquet de Pensées by Redouté. King George VI and Queen Elizabeth devoted a whole garden at Balmoral to this charming flower.

130

Bouquet de Pensées.

One of the Queen Mother's favourite spots: a wooden bench under the apple-scented rose 'Albertine', which is sheltered from the wind by honeysuckle- and clematis-covered trellis. Her Majesty loves seashells, and the paths here are strewn with them.

Edging the border and casting its scent about our path is *Alyssum maritima*; *Veronica spicata*, tall and blue, is by late August shedding its flowers, while the steely-blue, spiky flower-heads of *Echinops ritro*, the globe thistle, form a clump beside the mahogany-coloured *Helenium autumnale* 'Moerheim Beauty', thus forming a most effective composition in blue, rose and silver.

Continuing along the path we come to a barrier either side of the walk, made of rustic poles and chicken wire, fixed on top of more of those huge upright stone slabs. It runs from the wall, south to north, and is covered thickly with a late Dutch honeysuckle, *Lonicera periclymenum* 'Serotina'; some of the poles form an archway over the path and there is a similar barrier some yards further on, this one being covered with *Clematis orientalis* – the 'orange peel' clematis. The two barriers form an enclosure which Queen Elizabeth explains was made especially to give an extra sheltered area within the garden. A white-painted wooden seat is placed against the wall and a plant of the trusty rose 'Albertine' climbs above it, mingling with a fruiting cherry and a pear tree.

A riot of nasturtiums fills the narrow beds on either side of the seat and scrambles up the walls to a height of 6 feet, its grasping tentacles entangling a large-flowered blue-mauve hybrid clematis, 'Lasurstern'. Either side of the seat are two wooden tubs packed with deep blue and yellow violas, and in front of it is a loose and informal 'knot' of eleven small beds edged with *Sedum spurium*, a double and dwarf form of *Matricaria eximea* which has flowers the colour of Cornish cream, and further plants of *Alyssum maritima*. The roses that fill the beds are modern ones, given to Queen Elizabeth by Mr Cocker, the famous rose grower, and called 'Glenfiddich' after a whisky of that name – they are amber-yellow with dark foliage and are underplanted with petunias and some other low-growing annuals. But the Queen Mother's real favourites are the old-fashioned roses, and she has lately planted some of these in a narrow border under the flagged and trellised barrier facing west. The Alba rose × *incarnata*, 'Great Maiden's Blush', grown in gardens since at least the early eighteenth century, is here, also the Gallicas 'Assemblage des Beautés' and 'Tuscany Superb' (sometimes known as 'Old Velvet Rose'), and the moss roses 'Blanche Moreau' and 'William Lobb' ('Old Velvet Moss'), with its semi-double flowers

Left: The Queen Mother loves the old-fashioned roses such as the moss rose 'William Lobb' and is disappointed that they do not do well at Mey.
Right: The deep reddish-purple Gallica rose 'Tuscany Superb', another of Queen Elizabeth's favourite old-fashioned roses.

of deepest purple-crimson and its buds and fading flowers of ashy lavender. Alas, these beauties, much to Queen Elizabeth's disappointment, do not flourish – perhaps the soil, which is clay, does not suit them.

All the paths in this little garden are very white, and on looking closer you see why, for they are thickly covered with shells of many different kinds. The Queen Mother loves shells, admiring the beauty of their varied and wonderful patterns, and uses them for decoration in the house as well as the garden. Although it is an uncommon fancy nowadays to have shells on your garden paths, they were sometimes used in gardens in the seventeenth century, though not only for strewing on paths. Occasionally they lined the basins of fountains or the bottoms of canals in water parterres, and John Tradescant brought boxes of them back from his travels on the Continent for his master, Robert Cecil, and used them thus in the gardens at Hatfield. Among the many shells at Mey I saw no examples of the most famous shell in these parts, the 'groatie buckies', although I looked carefully for the tiny pinkish-white cowries which for 6,000 years have been threaded for necklaces and 'strings', made in exactly the same way today as they were at the dawn of Scottish history, and considered to bring good fortune.

Many herbaceous plants flourishing in this more sheltered part were here before Mr Webster's time and probably date back to 1920. *Phlox paniculata* does especially well, and also the *Penstemon barbatus* hybrids in pinks and reds. There are some very old michaelmas daisies still in bud in late August whose smoky-lavender flowers, small and old-fashioned, will later make the bushes look like wreaths of autumn mist.

Leaving this enclosure under the second archway you enter the north-west corner of the garden, and in the angle of the wall is a gazebo or pavilion, made of the same stone as the walls. It rises above them and has a window in the upper room from which you would be able to look out over the sea but the staircase leading to it is now too rickety to climb. The ground floor of the gazebo is the potting shed, and on the left there is a greenhouse which has plants grown chiefly for decoration in the castle. Here there are the fuchsias, 'Snowcap', 'C. J. Howlett' and 'Bon Accord' (a plant with pale and deep pink flowers), and *Nerine crispulum*, which will be in flower for Queen Elizabeth The Queen Mother's visit in October. There are also some begonias and pelargoniums in a mixture of colours, but chiefly pink, a colour much liked by Queen Elizabeth. Cinerarias are grown too, and coleus, lobelia and *Viola tricolor*, and in a second greenhouse, built against the wall and facing south, there is a dazzling display of pot plants. Many of the same plants seen in the first greenhouse are there, but

Opposite: Mr William Shearer, who helps in the garden at Mey, in the old gazebo (now used as a potting shed) which stands in the corner of the walled garden.

Above: The languorous fingers of a passion-flower add a romantic touch to the greenhouse. The green wall just visible is a mass of the rose- and lemon-scented pelargoniums which the Queen Mother loves.
Opposite: A rare sight these days: banked pots of pelargoniums, fuchsias, begonias and cineraria, edged with trailing lobelia, dazzle the visitor to the greenhouse.

here there are also maidenhair ferns and many plants of *Coleus blumei*, from Java, their leaves a fantasy of eastern colours – copper and emerald, bronze and apricot, pink and yellow; these are grown for the castle rooms, as are *Amaranthus tricolor* (Joseph's coat) and *Cuphea miniata* 'Firefly' with its bright cerise-red flowers. Basil is kept here for the chef, being too fragile for the garden even in August, and some pots of lily hybrids – 'Rosita', 'Medallion' and 'Rose

137

Fire' among them – which are a few of several sent up every year from London after Queen Elizabeth's birthday. But the greater number of the plants in this greenhouse are grown only for display – the whole being staged for August.

Since Queen Elizabeth bought the castle in 1952 she has chosen to cover the back wall of this greenhouse in a thick green curtain of sweet geranium – rose- and lemon-scented, for which she has a particular affection. In the area around the two houses (both of which are heated by electric fans) Mr Webster has his standing ground for the plants he raises, where they stay until they are ready to be planted out in the beds and borders; any spare plants are left here in case replacements should be needed. He grows all the bedding from seed and raises the plants in the two greenhouses, including the dahlias 'Coltness Gem', 'Dandy' and 'Caithness Jane', which often flower late into October, even surviving a degree or two of frost. There is a quantity of *Tagetes* 'Radio' here, not a popular flower with Queen Elizabeth, but in front of it there is a broad band of one she much admires, *Nemophila insignis* or baby blue-eyes, looking like a piece of Caribbean sky. Antirrhinums in single colours of orange,

Opposite: The true Victorian conservatory: *Il Penseroso* by John Atkinson Grimshaw, 1875.
Below: Nemophila insignis or baby blue-eyes is one of the annuals which delights Queen Elizabeth.

lavender, pink, yellow and red, as well as mixed colours, are there too, and catananche, that cornflower-like plant grown by the Elizabethans, as well as giant *Salpiglossis siniata*, their flowers etched in black on amazing shades of violet, scarlet, yellow, crimson and gold. These salpiglossis are used in the pattern of planting for those four borders in the garden filled completely with annuals. Ribbon bands of rainbow colours, they are planted with 'hedges' of sweet peas behind; then come the salpiglossis, next the antirrhinums and dahlias, and then, in front, fringed borders of blue lobelia and white alyssum.

Each year Mr Webster likes to try growing something new from seed, and this year it is *Catananche coerulea*, with its deep mauve semi-double flowers. A nursery bed, in this area near the greenhouses, holds cuttings of herbs and other more delicate plants, grown to replace those lost through 'wind burn'. I noticed a leptospermum and some borage, as well as tarragon and hyssop. Many herbs (perennial as well as annual) are also grown each year from seed, Mediterranean plants such as thyme never surviving the winter and always having to be raised afresh. In the third week in July the plants are set out in the 'herb bed' which lies under the wall that faces north. The herbs are much used in the castle kitchen and include chives and fennel, rosemary and dill, savory and borage, sorrel, mint and sage, besides Good King Henry, that admirable substitute for spinach, and quantities of Hamburg parsley. The herb bed suffers a good deal from the roots of the sycamore trees which grow the other side of the wall and steal the moisture from the soil, but rhubarb does well in a corner not far away, being cut and eaten in August, and lily-of-the-valley also flourishes here.

Beneath the east-facing wall of the garden the border has some caged blackcurrants – 'Ben Nevis' and 'Ben Lomond' – their leaves scenting the air, and some plants of *Stachys lanata* with its furry silver-grey leaves, as well as a quantity of Rugosa roses which flower very late in the year. Trained on the wall behind them are some espaliered apple trees, one with deep red fruit, and two fan-trained Victoria plums. Mr Webster explains that there is a shortage of bees to pollinate the fruit at blossom time, that the blossom quite often gets burned by the wind, that the fruit trees do best on the east wall, and that the cooking apples do better than the dessert varieties. Nevertheless it is quite a triumph to have any fruit at all to pick, as it is rare for apples to succeed north of Edinburgh.

Turning off the path into the centre of the garden, and moving from one enclosure, formed by the tapestry hedges, to another, we come to the vegetables. In the south-west are the peas – rows of them, all phased to be ready throughout the weeks of Queen Elizabeth's visits. Broad beans are here too, held steady by posts and wire, and some extra rows of sweet peas to provide

Opposite: The author admires the lush growth of annual lavatera, which lines the hedge in one of the soft fruit 'rooms' of the garden.

plenty for picking, for Queen Elizabeth is especially fond of them. Mr Webster plants the seeds in February, one seed each in old double-cream cartons – he pierces a hole in the bottom, puts in dead leaves and fills them up with a peat-based compost, which he finds makes for very good root growth. No opportunity is lost to grow flowers, and a bed opposite the peas is filled with Scotch marigolds and pink and white *Lavatera trimestris*, a hardy annual used for picking, which lasts well in water.

Above: Artichokes have long been valued as vegetables (this engraving is from John Parkinson's *Paradisus Terrestris*, 1629) but at Mey they are also an ornament in the garden; the Queen Mother is fond of their deeply cut architectural leaves.
Opposite: Redouté's *Groseiller Rouge*. The redcurrant bushes at Mey are 7–8 feet high and covered in fruit in August.

In an enclosure facing south-east there is a large bed full of globe artichokes. Queen Elizabeth thinks they came from France many years ago, before Her Majesty came to Mey. Their huge, purple-shadowed, silvery green pom-poms are especially good eating, and their stiff, deeply cut architectural leaves are also much admired by Queen Elizabeth and are an ornament in the garden. To keep them going they need dividing in April and a heavy feeding every third year, with manure coming from the Royal Farm. Both the manure and another

Groseiller rouge.   *Ribes rubrum.*

fertilizer, Vitax Q4, are given generously to other plants as well, and spread over the garden as quantities allow, while a certain amount of peat is bought in to use for a top dressing, after a disastrous experience with peat given by a neighbour. This came from the bottom of an old peat bank, and when it was put on the garden everything turned brown and died. It seems there was phosphorus in it. 'I might have guessed,' said the neighbour when told of the devastation. 'When we burn the peat our ash is always yellow!'

Flowers complement vegetables in many of the enclosures. A square of gladioli faces a rolling line of sea-green cabbages (buried under nets to keep off the marauding pigeons); the bright green feathery tops of carrots oppose a bed packed with the massed yellow flowers of *Helenium* 'Autumn Butterpat'. Other enclosures hold neat rows of beetroot, turnips, parsnip and swedes, and in one there is almost a little field of vivid green parsley, with the contrasting perpendicular and round shapes of cos and cabbage lettuces beside it.

A fruit cage holds gooseberries and redcurrants, the latter 7–8 feet high with trunks 10 inches in circumference, and laden with fruit; Elsa Sutherland, who works at Mey in the summer helping Mr Webster (and who is shortly to work at Windsor Castle), has come to pick over the great bushes and carries a bowl already half full of the shining ripe fruit. They must be very old, these currants, as indeed are the gooseberries, both dessert and cooking varieties, for it is said they were planted in 1953. The strawberries are old too, the original plants having been given to the place in 1926 by a gamekeeper from Morayshire, and were much favoured by the Queen Mother for their sweetness and flavour and their continuous fruiting even into August, but now, sadly, they have a virus and are being replaced by other varieties. What a constitution they must have had, though, to thrive for so many years!

Cauliflowers are grown as well, but like the cabbages have to be protected by nets from the ravages of wood-pigeons. Onions look after themselves, while the leeks with their blue-grey leaves sit in orderly ranks and the potato 'Duke of York', grown large by the month of August, will soon be ready to feed the household. Raspberries, usually thriving in Scotland, do not do well here, but Aberdeen's Macaulay Institute has tested the soil and found that it contains too much lime. Some years ago shale from a nearby beach was put into the soil to the depth of 3 inches to help work the clay, but it can still be seen undecomposed at the top of the beds, and is thought to have adversely affected the raspberries. Now new canes have been planted, with liberal quantities of peat around them, and 'Malling Jewel' and 'Malling Promise' have replaced the old 'Norfolk Giant' and 'Glen Clova'.

The path which leads past the raspberry bed carries us to the border under the west-facing wall, and although it is a garden where plants are sensibly being 'repeated', once they have been found able to stand the special conditions, in this

The Queen Mother is well qualified to judge a juicy home-grown strawberry!

border there are several we have not seen before. The tall *Solidago canadensis* 'Lemore' is here, *Sedum spectabile* 'Autumn Joy', much loved by butterflies, *Lysimachia clethroides* with spikes of blush-white flowers, and some day lilies (hemerocallis). To the front of the bed are two hostas, 'Royal Standard' with milk-white scented flowers, and *H. albo-pilosa tardiana*. The hosta, or funkia as it used to be called, was found in Japan by Robert Fortune in the nineteenth century, and has become, nearly a century and a half later, the most fashionable of plants with its fine leaves in a great variety of size and colour, some nearly blue, others gold and green or white and green, others still dark green or even a

chartreuse colour. It is planted largely for its leaves, which with their strong bold outlines give the necessary firm contrasts in beds or borders.

Wood-pigeons have been mentioned as a pest in the garden, playing havoc, if allowed to get away with it, among the cauliflowers and cabbage; netting the vegetables deals with this problem, but a more trying pest and one more difficult to control is the rabbit. Usually they can be kept out of the walled garden, but a gate was left open and a doe rabbit made her way in and had six young. Mr Webster, playing 'Mr McGregor', finds Peter Rabbit hard to catch, but the corgis Ranger and Dash on their walks with the Queen Mother have accounted for three.

I think of John Evelyn's advice in his *Sylva* of 1664 on tasks to be done at different seasons of the year – 'in January (as in December) continue your hostility against vermin' – and this Mr Webster certainly does with vigour and energy; but hunting rabbits is only one of several winter jobs, and he busies himself with things like walling and repairs during the months when there is little real gardening to do. He works single-handed from October to March apart from help from Mr William Shearer, a native of the northernmost tip of Caithness who has helped in the garden at Mey for six years. It is clearly no easy task to care for this garden; patience as well as skill is needed, and a philosophical outlook and much optimism, if a gardener is to succeed when nature produces conditions far from ideal for growing plants. Lack of moisture and the remorseless wind in the gardens at Mey are certain at times to bring disappointment, but over many years Queen Elizabeth and her gardener have learned from their failures and have always been willing to try again.

You come away from this garden with the feeling – thoroughly reinforced – that you had with your first glimpse of it – that here there has most surely been a triumph of will, and skill, over the uncontrollable and capricious forces of nature. Man has succeeded against formidable odds (away from the meadows, the ocean and the woods) in creating a symbol of safety and pleasure, an enclosed garden or 'hortus conclusus' which to medieval man was a vision of Paradise.

As I turn to leave the garden through the gate by which I entered, the impressions I carry away are of a place that fulfils all the purposes for which it was created. Looking here and there a little like a Beatrix Potter watercolour, it has an atmosphere of charming homeliness – unpretentious and yet pleasing, fitting perfectly into the setting of the pretty castle that it exists to serve, visible from every point within the walls that surround, like comforting arms, a place where peace and plenty can be found.

Opposite: A view from the castle of one of the vegetable 'rooms' in the garden, with the Pentland Firth in the distance.

Birkhall

DEESIDE

Although it is a fair day in May, the snow is still lying in patches on the hills as I travel down the valley of the river Dee, the road winding and curving as it follows the river through first the small town of Aboyne and then that of Ballater, with its church spire rising among the houses strung along the far bank.

The road takes me to the left, and after a mile or two I enter a drive by a simple white-painted gate leading through undulating land with trees of immense height, their boles branchless for many feet – there are Scots pines, oak, beech, various other conifers, and quantities of birch. The woodland here has little or no undergrowth, except for the luxuriant, curving fronds of tall-stemmed ferns, but the earth is covered with a brilliant moss, shaded in many different greens, which spreads over the broken ground of depressions, dells, smoothly undulating mounds, shelves and lumps like a verdant sea, engulfing huge rocks and stones and sweeping up the hill to vanish into the dark shadows of the wood.

I have already caught sight of the house from the road – for a moment only it comes into view and then it vanishes behind a screen of trees, but I have had time to notice how high it stands and that it is a white house with tree-covered hills on either side of it, and others beyond. It now comes more fully into view as I round another bend in the drive, and I can see that its windows are white-painted and sashed, with rectangular panes of glass.

Opposite: Her Majesty's gardens at Birkhall on Royal Deeside reflect the simple charm and welcoming atmosphere of this holiday home.

The long drive begins to open out as I near the house, and there is the glimpse of a stream, known as the Fountain Burn, rushing between sloping banks retained by granite pavé – there have recently been heavy rains. On the far side of the stream a delicate fringe, lightly and openly planted, of birch, Scots pine, elder and hazel rises from cropped grass.

Further down, the meandering stream is spanned here and there by simple wooden bridges, one of planks with no hand-rail and one narrow and railed – cross one of these and I am in a closely planted wood. The banks of the stream on this side have a fringe of *Rhododendron ponticum*, low and bushy, not showing any of its usual invasive vigour; climate and conditions probably control its growth, which in lusher, less harsh areas can become almost impossible to suppress.

Bright velvety moss covers the roots of birches and conifers in the nearby woodland.

Queen Elizabeth fishing with her gillie in the river Dee during her spring visit.

The grassy bank wanders close to the stream and then wanders away. Here dog's mercury and carex grow, the latter with a large coarse leaf, and the many greens of the abundant foliage are sobered by the white flowers of the delicate wood anemone. A spreading clump of Scots pines wanders up the hill out of a dell, and on the far left, beyond them, are fir and larch woods – the larch trees a tender green in spring and butter gold in autumn, their boughs curving gracefully upwards, furnished with drooping branchlets below.

Growing on the bank of the stream I have just left is a noble oak, its huge branches rising to a great height, while near to it is a fine birch burdened with lichen. Through them, and over the stream, can be seen the tumbling, coursing broken waters of the river Muick, brown as brown ale, with froth, white and cream, planing up shavings of crystal spray on its troubled surface, and carrying its water into the great river Dee from which, in the month of May, Queen Elizabeth The Queen Mother will be pulling the fresh-run silver salmon. For Queen Elizabeth loves her fishing. All her life she has been a keen and highly

A watercolour of 1849 by William Henry Fisk in the Queen's collection. It shows the main Queen Anne section of Birkhall before the Queen Mother added a wing to the left of the house.

The Duke of York was a very fine shot, and in August Birkhall would be filled with friends invited up to Scotland for the grouse season. *Grouse Flying over the Moor* by George Edward Lodge.

skilful fisherman, and it is to Birkhall, in the spring of the year, that she comes to indulge for a little while in her favourite sport.

The house now is fully in view, its front door scarcely visible beneath a large porch with its roof supported by pillars of silver-grey painted oak trunks from the neighbouring estate of Abergeldie, with the nodes and stumps of small severed branches still on them; there are four of these great pillars, and the walls of the house, bold and white, rise behind them.

Its aspect is neither pompous nor grand, indeed the simplicity of its architecture gives it an air of comely homeliness, at once friendly and welcoming, its window panes catching the light of the westering sun. The grey tiles of the roof carry a fluff of silvery-green lichen and moss which softens the severity and darkness of the slate.

Most of the building we see from here is comparatively new, for much has been added to the original small Queen Anne house over the years. The Queen Mother, when she came to Birkhall in 1952, was making a return to a house that she had lived in a great deal as Duchess of York. Birkhall became a favourite holiday home when she and the Duke, with the two Princesses, Elizabeth and Margaret, used to come here in August for the grouse shooting on the moors

153

and later, in the early autumn, for the partridge and pheasant shooting in the woods and fields about the house. The Duke was, like his father George V, a very fine shot, and Birkhall would be filled with guests; many happy days were spent on the heather-covered hills, and by the side of Loch Muick, the lake high and hidden on the moors, where they could picnic in peace and privacy. The Duchess was as skilled with a fly-rod as the Duke was with a gun; in May, when the salmon were running in the river Dee, they would come here for the fishing, and during these visits plans would be drawn up for additions and improvements to the house as well as the garden. Apple trees were imported, herbaceous borders enlarged, and fresh plantings made, while the two young Princesses held many tea parties in their summerhouse.

But the main alteration to the house was carried out when the present Queen gave Birkhall to her mother after King George VI died. In 1952 a new L-shaped wing was added, the lower floor of which was a large drawing-room with French windows opening on to the garden – a flight of steps descends from them and a narrow but delightful view can be glimpsed, through a wrought-iron gate of grapes and vine leaves over the river to the fields and moors beyond. The upper storey of the new wing contains extra bedrooms for guests, and the end of the wing is bowed so that the windows catch the light from several quarters, making the rooms bright and sunny. The addition has been done with a skill that makes the harmony of new and old most satisfying to the eye; and the white walls and grey slates of the new building blend imperceptibly with those of the ancient house.

Left: The Queen Mother's guests can spend a happy hour or two quietly fishing on Loch Muick; the river Muick runs right through the garden at Birkhall.
Right: Queen Elizabeth and the author's father-in-law, the late Marquess of Salisbury, enjoy a picnic on the moor above Birkhall (September 1960).

Left: A hedge of × *Cupressocyparis leylandii* is an essential windbreak but allows a view over the fields to the little town of Ballater.

Right: One of the vistas offers a glimpse of the tumbling waters of the river Muick among the trees and, in the distance, the moorland over which Queen Elizabeth, like Queen Victoria before her, walks in all weathers.

It is essential, if we are to understand and appreciate the character and ambience of a place like Birkhall, to search a little into its past history, to know something about the people who have lived there and the events that have occurred. These things, inextricably enmeshed with the creations of nature, cast a glow or a gloom and are the springheads of its atmosphere and spirit.

We know little about the history of the area before the old house was built, although we do know that the Romans arrived here and settled about the valley of the Dee, as there are traces of their roads to be found. Hundreds of years later we can imagine the wild and primitive life of the clans and their leaders who occupied the stone castles such as Crathes (in modern times famous for its remarkable garden), which abounded in the region. The north-east Highlands never really succumbed to the imposed feudalism that affected other areas of the

Highlands, and the clans continued to scrape a rather uncomfortable living well into the seventeenth century. In the eighteenth century the system began to break up when the clansmen supported Bonnie Prince Charlie in the 1745 rebellion. One of the supporters of the Jacobite rising in 1715, albeit a far from ardent one, was the owner of Birkhall, Captain Charles Gordon, who made a living from the 6,500 acres surrounding the property; he married his cousin, Rachel Gordon of Abergeldie, whose lands marched with those of Birkhall and who had inherited the castle from her brother. The barony of Abergeldie had been granted to her ancestor Alexander Seton by James II of Scotland, and the property of Birkhall went with the barony. Its name derives from 'birk ha', which is a Celtic description of the birch trees, many of which can still be seen in the plantings surrounding the house; their silvery-white trunks and graceful outlines are much loved by Queen Elizabeth, and they help to cut some of the cold winds of winter.

Rachel Gordon built the plain, unpretentious house of the local granite, with a roof of slates brought from Meall Dudn, a nearby quarry, and proudly placed an inscription of the date, 1715, and her own and her husband's initials over the front door when she had finished the building. When Charles and Rachel Gordon died, Birkhall became the home of their third son, Joseph, a much more ardent supporter of the Jacobite cause than his father had been. He fought at the battle of Culloden, taking some of his clansmen with him, and after the defeat there of Bonnie Prince Charlie he had to hide himself to escape capture; this he did near to his home at Birkhall. Meanwhile his wife, Eliza, harboured the fugitive Oliphants of Gask, who disguised themselves as 'Mr Whytt' and 'Mr Brown', writing under these names to their ladies in Perthshire; for twenty years they kept this guise, and we can imagine how miserable those years of fear and subterfuge must have been – as he waited for the gallows the eldest Oliphant made out a will leaving all he possessed to his hostess Eliza Gordon – it reads thus:

> Delivered to Mrs Gordon at Birkhall: A sute of Highland cloaths and Phylibeg, A coarse nightgown, a Buff coloured weastcoat with fold buttons, A pair red everlasting britches. Two pair pistols, a shabble with hart-horn hilt, mounted with silver, a Hatt with the gold tracing that was upon it. A pair Silver buckles; all left with her in a cloch-bag.

He might well have been deeply grateful to Mrs Gordon, for not only had she risked much to save his life and that of his kinsman, but she finally managed to plan the escape to Sweden of the wretched traitor on 10 November 1746.

Opposite: The name of Birkhall derives from the fine birch trees which surround it, typical of the Highland landscape. *Sheep Grazing beneath a Birch Tree* by John Macwhirter.

Balmoral, Her Majesty's Highland Residence, a watercolour by John Henry Mole of 1853. It was Prince Albert who originally purchased Birkhall, which is within walking distance of Balmoral, for the young Prince of Wales.

After these stirring and dramatic years Birkhall seems to have receded into quiet anonymity for several decades, to emerge in the nineteenth century when Prince Albert's eye fell on it, envisaging it as the ideal Scottish home for his eldest son, the Prince of Wales. He purchased it, and its estate, from the Fife trustees three years before he succeeded in purchasing Balmoral, although it had been leased by the Queen for some time. This was in the year 1849, when the Prince of Wales was only eight years old, and in fact he stayed here only once, the house usually being occupied by friends of Queen Victoria and various of her courtiers. Among those who came to stay was Florence Nightingale, much to the pleasure and excitement of the Queen, to whom she was a great heroine; the Queen's excitement was even greater when she learnt she was to come straight from Scutari to Birkhall, for she would be able to hear first-hand news from the field of battle. Florence and her father came and stayed there with Sir James Clark, a loyal and much-loved member of the household who was then occupying the house.

Queen Victoria loved Deeside and the hills and lochs that surrounded it, and was never happier than when at Balmoral. She would take long walks and arrange picnics, accompanied by friends, on the hillside or on the moors above Birkhall, which was only eight miles from the castle (her great favourite, the gillie John Brown, came from the topmost loch in the river Muick). The Queen was marvellously indifferent to the cold, and in spite of it being an age when people were undoubtedly hardier than we are in the late twentieth century, Balmoral was famous for its chill – even Czar Nicholas II complained of the cold when staying there.

The Queen occupied herself with various works too, and besides the complete rebuilding of Balmoral Castle, she diverted the road from Royal Deeside by building a bridge by Crathie Kirk which has proved a blessing to the Royal Family in later years, enhancing their privacy when they take their holidays there.

It was Queen Victoria and Prince Albert who were the first to set the tradition, which has carried on over the years down to our present day, of providing generous employment in the area, both in the royal houses and in maintaining the shooting over the moors and in the woods and the fishing in the river Dee. When Prince Albert died Queen Victoria retreated to Scotland, finding comfort and consolation in the quiet seclusion of her Highland home. Her virtual disappearance from public view attracted a great deal of adverse criticism, and her popularity waned as her retirement became more and more complete. One of her most loved places was a small cottage at the head of Loch Muick, and she would spend many days there, living in a most simple way, sketching, writing her journal and riding her Highland pony, accompanied only by a few members of her household, friends and her gillie John Brown. It would have pleased her greatly if the Prince of Wales had come to live in the charming house his father had bought for him, but her elder son did not care for Birkhall; he complained that it was too small and uncomfortable and, much to

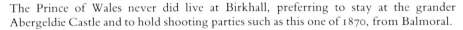

The Prince of Wales never did live at Birkhall, preferring to stay at the grander Abergeldie Castle and to hold shooting parties such as this one of 1870, from Balmoral.

Anglers on the Dee near Balmoral by Alfred de Breanski. Fishing is one of the main attractions of Deeside for the Royal Family.

the Queen's disappointment and annoyance, he used to rent Abergeldie Castle which he found much more to his taste. Abergeldie, which dates from 1430, has been occupied by members of the Royal Family for over a hundred years, being rented on a long lease from the Gordon family. Only three miles from Balmoral and lying east of the castle, it used to have a beautiful Elizabethan garden. Today it is the home of Mr John Gordon, a descendant of the Gordons who built Birkhall.

The Queen reluctantly accepted that the Prince would never live at Birkhall, and in 1885 she decided to buy it from him so as to keep it in royal hands, letting it to the young widow of her son, Prince Leopold, who had died a haemophiliac when only thirty-one. Princess Helena, Duchess of Albany, was left with two small children, the elder of whom, Princess Alice – later to be wife of the Earl of Athlone – has given us a vivid picture of domestic life in Queen Victoria's household, and leaves us a delightful vignette of her childhood days at Birkhall:

> Here we spent some of the happiest days of our lives. It was a small place in those days. We loved the sloping garden full of fruit and sweet-peas, and at the bottom, a chain bridge, heavenly to jump upon, which spanned the rushing little Muick, where we loved to play.

And so it has continued at Birkhall to the present day – the pleasures which are to be had there at certain seasons, in the happiness of a house which has been loved as a family home over the long years. In May, a month full of promise, there are days to be spent on the river Dee, throwing a fly into the bright waters, and in the fullness of August Queen Elizabeth The Queen Mother can, like Queen Victoria before her, picnic on the heather-covered hills or indulge in the enjoyments of her garden when it is at its peak. On early autumn days, when the leaves are turning scarlet and gold, later to fall dishevelled upon the earth – green and yellow and pale brown – Her Majesty will walk her dogs among the flowers and vegetables or through the woods around the house, taking particular pleasure in what she has created and in the beauty of the surrounding country.

When the Duke of York succeeded to the throne on the abdication of his brother Edward VIII, he and the Duchess, now George VI and Queen Elizabeth, had to move to Balmoral. Although they had the interest of making several changes to the garden there, opening up vistas to the river Dee and making a delightful formal garden filled with pansies, it must have been with some regret that they left the simple charms of Birkhall and the peace and contentment they had found there.

When the Second World War broke out in 1939, there was some fear for the safety of the Princesses and they were sent to Birkhall with their governess for a short time. The house was used again in 1947, when Princess Elizabeth, who had married Prince Philip of Greece, came here for a brief part of her honeymoon.

Having explored its past for a moment, I must now return to what is the true object of my visit to Birkhall, the discovery of the gardens which surround and embellish the house today. These are, like the house itself, neither particularly large nor particularly grand, but share several characteristics with those of the Queen Mother's other homes.

The setting of Birkhall is superb: the garden is on a slope which offers open views over river, fields and moorland, yet a mantle of woodland ensures complete privacy and shelter from the wind. As I noted from my approach, clever planting on the outer limits of the garden enables it to blend easily with the natural beauty that surrounds it; and, as at the Castle of Mey in Caithness, Birkhall has an eclectic mixture of flowers, fruit and vegetables which gives it something of the atmosphere of an old-fashioned cottage garden. It is not to be wondered at that Queen Elizabeth The Queen Mother spends so much time in it, climbing and descending the paths and steps, exercising her corgis and taking a close interest in the plants and flowers, discussing with her head gardener Mr James Kerr their choice and arrangement.

Much of the beauty of the garden at Birkhall must be credited to Mr Kerr, who devotes all his energies to making the garden look its best for the Queen Mother. He is a smiling, greying man in his early sixties who was once a dairy farmer but who has worked in the garden here at Birkhall for seventeen years. His wife runs a Bed and Breakfast from their house in Ballater. Mr Kerr's careful cultivations and discriminating care are to be noticed in every part of the garden and he has one full-time helper, Mr Murray, who works in the garden from March to November and helps with indoor work on the estate during the winter.

As we stand at the front of Birkhall, we see that the ground slopes away to the left beyond the drive and gravel sweep before the building. Here the grass begins, and spreads to a border 8 feet wide and 250 feet long, planted in blocks of varying sizes, but mostly 4–5 feet wide. It is planted with magnificent groups of herbaceous plants, all of which flower late in the season so that there should

Opposite above: The author with Birkhall's gardener, Mr James Kerr, who has cared for the garden for over sixteen years.
Opposite below: A striking feature of the garden is the 250-foot-long herbaceous border (seen here behind a large lime tree) which winds around its perimeter.
Left: The helmet-like flowers of *Aconitum napellus* – one of the plants forming 4-foot blocks of colour in the border.
Right: The scent of *Cardiocrinum giganteum*, towering 10 or 12 feet high at the back of the border, is especially strong as you stroll around the garden on a warm summer's evening.

be the best show possible for Her Majesty's stay during late summer and autumn.

There is massed *Aconitum napellus*, with its deeply cut leaves and purple-blue flowers looking like little helmets; *Lythrum virgatum*, with its rose-purple flowers in graceful spikes. Un-named varieties of *Phlox paniculata* are here too, casting their nut-like scent on the air, with blocks of marigolds and golden rod, though there is not a great deal of the latter as Queen Elizabeth does not care for it; preferred are groups of that delicious old-fashioned plant, *Nepeta* × *faassenii* or 'catmint', so called because it is believed that cats love rolling in it – and who shall blame them, for it has a warm inviting smell of hot spiciness. Its flowers are a soft lavender, and it is altogether more desirable than and superior to its coarse hybrid 'Six Hills Giant', as different as a wrestler is to a ballet dancer.

Next there is a block of *Achillea filipendulina* with its yellow flower-heads, flat as pancakes and a mustardy yellow, the leaves a good foil to the flowers, for they are a gentle grey-green, feathery and fern-like. Michaelmas daisies crowd into a square – these are some of the more old-fashioned kinds, with misty colours, like the smoke from autumn bonfires. There is a tall plant called *Ligularia dentata* with deep yellow daisy flowers, its leaf shaped like a coltsfoot, and some kniphofias (red hot pokers) which were brought here from the Castle of Mey some three years ago, a tall, very red variety.

Tiger lilies have been planted too, and they do extremely well at Birkhall, but they are one of the very few late summer flowers that are over by August, so they are seldom able to give pleasure to the Queen Mother with their orange-red Turk's-cap flowers, spotted with purple-black, and their anthers covered in darkest red pollen. The tiger lily's native home is in the far east – Korea, China and Japan – where its bulbs have been cultivated and grown commercially for more than 2,000 years. It came first to this country early in the nineteenth century and was known then as the Chinese Lily, and cottagers loved to plant it in their gardens, where it was supremely happy in the always well worked and humus-rich soil of the cottage garden. Alas, the bulb is now a victim of several viruses and it is rare these days to see it growing as robustly as it does at Birkhall.

One of the most spectacular plants in this part of the garden is another member of the Liliaceae family, a native of Assam and the Himalayas – *Cardiocrinum giganteum*; towering to 10 or 12 feet, with heart-shaped leaves of shining green, its flowers are funnels of snowy white, with throats stained with purple and shaded with green on their outsides. There are sometimes more than twenty flowers to a stem, their fragrance so intense that it can be noticed many yards away and, should you be strolling in the garden on a calm summer night, their sweetness is then especially strong.

This great winding border, like a huge colourful snake, is backed by a narrow band of grass and behind that is a planting of beech, birch, chamaecyparis, a row

This richly coloured floribunda rose, 'Glenfiddich' (*left*), is grown in beds in the lawn along with the canary yellow 'Honeymoon' (*right*), which was planted after Princess Alexandra spent part of her honeymoon here at Birkhall.

of five sycamores and some snowberry (an old inhabitant of this country, arriving early in the eighteenth century from the United States; its flowers, tiny and pink and looking like little urns, turn later into clusters of glistening white berries). All these plants form a broken hedge at the back of the border, and they play a valuable part in cutting the wind in this area.

In the 1890s to 1900s, the Queen's Keeper of the Privy Purse, Sir Dighton Probyn, lived at Birkhall, and it is thought that he made the great border; certainly many of the plants in it are old varieties whose names have been lost in the mists of time. The plants in it are divided up in a three-year rotation and, depending on the weather, it takes six weeks to split and re-plant the year's third.

Cut in the grass between the big border and the drive are beds shaped like salad plates – crescents filled with roses, except for two which are waiting to be planted up with annuals. The roses are hybrid tea and floribundas: 'Glenfiddich', called after the famous whisky of that name by Mr Cocker, the raiser, and 'Honeymoon', a canary yellow rose with deeper buds which is a great flowerer. The latter was planted after Princess Alexandra spent part of her honeymoon here after her marriage to Mr Angus Ogilvy.

The roses are thoroughly dressed each year with well-rotted farmyard manure and an organic fertilizer, Vitax Q4 organic – no chemical fertilizers are used in the gardens at all, as Queen Elizabeth does not like them on the flowers or vegetables. The soil is acid, rather poor and sandy, and Mr Kerr says that it needs these heavy doses of manure to keep it in good heart (as well as liming every five years); I saw a large heap of it by the back gate in the spring, waiting to be given to the hungry garden. Leaf-mould is also used to build up the humus in the soil, and Mr Kerr tries to get as much as possible collected before the snow sets in. Sometimes he uses a little systemic fungicide but he does not think it does a great deal of good.

Insect pests and diseases are not troublesome here, perhaps because of the climate, and there are no invasions of greenfly. On the other hand rabbits are a problem – they appear to be immune to myxomatosis – and the roe deer are a great nuisance, especially in the winter when the cold and snow drive them to seek somewhere where they can find greater shelter and some food; as a result some wiring has to be done to try and keep out these troublesome beasts.

At the end of the great border, nearest to the entrance front of the house, with its back to the wood and with a very fine yew tree nearby, is a charming little wooden house – the 'Wendy House'. Bought at the Inverness Highland Show many years ago, it is made of 'rustic' wooden planks with the bark left on the outside, its roof thatched with heather, the roof-ridge clad with clods of earth. Although it is seldom used now, in the days when the Princesses Elizabeth and Margaret Rose came to Birkhall with their parents in the spring, and in the late summer and autumn, it was one of the summerhouses in which they played and held tea parties; a perfect setting for the fanciful games of childhood.

To the right and left of the front door are narrow borders, planted in spring with mixed tulips and narcissus with an edging of polyanthus. The latter are regularly divided, and in spite of always being planted back in the same place they have never had any disease; perhaps this is because they are the old-fashioned type with smaller flowers – the modern, large-flowered varieties, which have the blood of those more fragile hybrids from the western United States, are very subject to virus troubles, and can seldom be planted more than two years running in the same place. Certainly the constitution of the polyanthus has been impaired by over-sizing and over-breeding and, beautiful as the modern ones are with their rainbow colours, the older ones have a great deal to recommend them.

The spring bedding in these borders is followed by a planting of mixed zonal pelargoniums, which are grown from seed and are much liked by Queen Elizabeth. Against the house walls are three roses carefully pruned and tied, their names unknown. These roses have been here for many years, and the labels have long ago been lost.

Left: The chain bridge over the river Muick. Princess Alice used to love to bounce on it when she lived at Birkhall as a child.
Right: The heather-thatched 'Wendy House' where many years ago the Princesses Elizabeth and Margaret used to hold tea parties.

If we follow the length of the border, it will lead us to the south garden, which lies 100 feet below the house and is the main flower and vegetable garden. Its unique form, shaped like a bell, is outlined by a low hedge of white-flowered heath which is clipped firmly in April; this particular year, however, the weather has been extremely cold and it is still unclipped, but Mr Kerr will soon be putting the shears to it. The beds it outlines are planted with vegetables and very beautiful they are – cabbages rolling in precise military line, their fecund blue-grey or lime-green outlines a foil for the brilliant emerald of the curly kale, surely one of the most spectacular greens in the vegetable kingdom. Here utility bears sway, but it is coupled with an old-time beauty, at once homely and serviceable; the house is supplied with all the vegetables and fruit it needs,

Above: The bell-shaped garden has a gentle note of formality, which combines with an abundance of flowers in a manner reminiscent of many of the great gardens of Scotland. *Opposite:* Flowers and vegetables are grown decoratively together, a Scottish tradition also followed by the Queen Mother at the Castle of Mey.

which during the times when the Queen Mother is at home is a considerable amount, if they are to be sufficient for all the household and the guests also. Because Birkhall is 600 feet above sea level the crops are, on the whole, earlier than in other places in the region. So we find a small field of carrots, neat rows of leeks, beetroot with red-fringed leaves and a goodly patch of the humble potato, besides onions and the clotted heads of cauliflower. Herbs are here too – lovage with its celery-flavoured leaves and seeds, excellent for stews and soups; tarragon (which has to have protection in the winter) and mint – and here are the raspberries ('Zeva', which ripens at the end of August) set in five rows, and making a most excellent stuffing for grouse, as well as a delicious dessert.

Phlox paniculata 'Windsor' lines either side of the path down the centre of the garden like two wide pink ribbons.

But besides the vegetables and fruit there are many flowers in this bell-shaped garden, for the planting is in the true tradition of old Scottish gardens, with all the qualities of usefulness and charm combined. As George Eliot described a similar garden:

> . . . it was one of those old-fashioned paradises which hardly exist any longer except as memories of our childhood. No finical separation between flowers and kitchen garden there; no monotony of enjoyment for one sense to the exclusion of another . . .

There are roses, a *mélange* of hybrid teas, and here in beds alongside the path and almost 100 yards long, *Phlox paniculata* 'Windsor' is grown, the plants packed

A thick clipped beech hedge protects the plants on the western boundary. The outline of the 'bell', marked by an edging of white heath, is on the right.

close to make a 6-foot-wide ribbon of colour like a pink sash on a party frock – then a sudden outcrop of rhubarb, in April under forcing pots, so as to have it ready for the Queen Mother's visit in May. At the back of the ribbon of phlox there are taut double wires, 6 feet high, along which will be put brashings of larch from the woods; these will be turned later into a hedge of sweet peas – pale and bright pinks, hazy blues, white and creams – which are left to grow as they will, to be picked and taken into the house in great bunches. In contrast, behind the potting shed, there is a row of sweet peas – what Mr Kerr calls 'good sweet peas' – grown on high wires, tied and trained, their tendrils removed, to be cut for very special vases for the house.

The sweet pea (*Lathyrus odoratus*) is a native of southern Europe and Asia Minor. Its deliciously scented deep claret purple and mauve flowers were first grown in England in the late seventeenth century. A Dr Robert Uvedale, who was the headmaster of a grammar school at Enfield in Middlesex and a remarkable plantsman, grew sweet peas among the many exotic plants in his gardens and greenhouses. It was written of him that 'his flowers were choice, his stock numerous, and his culture of them very methodical and curious'. When he died in 1722 his plant collection was sold to Sir Robert Walpole at Houghton Hall in Norfolk. Since those days amazing things have happened to the sweet pea. In 1870 a man called Henry Eckford began to cross them and developed many new strains; several nurserymen copied his example, including the one who bred the famous Spencer hybrids. Modern sweet peas have more flowers to a stem, and the stems are longer and stronger, the flowers larger, and the number of colours, and shades of colours, immense. Many are still sweet-scented, but the astonishing fragrance of the small pre-Spencer varieties and the humble Sicilian wild flower has been lost. Now once more the pre-Spencer varieties can be grown, and very delicious they are, with flowers in colours that blend perfectly with the old-fashioned roses and pinks, and with the same amazing scent.

Turning to face south at this point, I see a tall iron pergola which must once have been clothed with roses; it is angled to lead on to a bridge no longer there, and seems to hold up the evergreens arching above it, forming a bosky shadowed walk from which I step out into the light and sun and on to a graceful narrow chain bridge, suspended and spanning the river – the bridge of Princess Alice's happy memories of her childhood days. It sways gently as I step on to it, and on my May visit (with the spring rains and the melted snows) the rushing, tumbling waters of the river, so closely visible through the slate of the bridge beneath my feet, give a feeling of imbalance and insecurity; my ears are filled with the noise of the waters, as I look down at the flying movement of the stream.

Along the edge of the water, with their roots well in it, are hazels and geans (the wild cherry, *Prunus avium*), and by the bridge is a large holly tree. Leaning out over the waters, there is a beech whose young green leaves appear at much the same time as the first flowers of the cherries. Mr Kerr tells me of the winter of 1980, when the river was completely frozen over and you could walk across the 3-foot-deep ice. Most winters here are not especially severe, however, although during 1985–6 much snow fell and the garden had a blanket of white late into the spring, warmly protecting the plantings from the severe frost that followed.

Opposite: Hedges of sweet peas are grown up brashings of larch and are used in large informal bunches for the house. The old-fashioned varieties are much more fragrant than the large modern hybrids. Illustration by Redouté, from *Choix des plus belles Fleurs.*

Pois de senteur.   *Lathyrus odoratus.*

P. J. Redouté.   Langlois.

There are misconceptions about the weather in Scotland, and travellers have been heard to utter unkind things about the climate which, I suppose, has been much the same for the last 1,000 years. It is often believed that it is a great deal wetter than in England and Wales, and that its winters are more severe; this is not so, except in the case of western Scotland, which is wetter, and the high ground, which does have more snow. However, generally speaking the winters are no more severe than they are in England. Here at Birkhall there is sometimes a late spring frost, and the first frosts of autumn are usually in October, white and often heavy. In one eccentric year recently, though, there were three frosts in August which killed all the petunias, dahlias and marigolds. There is not a great deal of wind.

Leaving the bridge, we make our return to the garden. In the summer months annuals are planted in broad bands within the small hedge of white heath that outlines it – asters and antirrhinums, godetias and other old-fashioned 'cottagey' flowers. Nearby there is an edging of alpine strawberries; these were killed in the great frost of 1985–6 and are martyrs to the mice, but in normal years they are easy and hardy, fruiting the first year if grown from seed, which is the best way to raise them.

Surveying the garden from here, we see that it is not quite symmetrical, rising like the palm of a cupped hand – or a concave fan – at times quite steeply, coming to a stop under a greystone wall which supports the terrace. It is bounded on the west by a clipped beech hedge, rounded at the top and hung with Titian-tawny leaves in the winter months until these are overcome by the fresh green of its young growth. The hedge is clipped in July and is not repeated on the eastern boundary of the garden, where instead the bounds are indicated only by the occasional plants of various evergreens, beech and snowberry behind the border, the spaces between them allowing a view through to the river and the landscape beyond.

The wall of grey granite supporting the terrace is about 6 feet tall and has a narrow border running along the full length of its top, planted with more *Lythrum virgatum* and clumps of *Colchicum autumnale*. Leafless when in flower, this autumn crocus's leaves appear in spring and die in summer before the flowers appear – a shining bright green; it is called after the Armenian city of Colchis, the birthplace of Medea and known for its poisonous plants, where it grew abundantly. Horace wrote of '. . . every baleful juice which poisonous Colchian globes produce'. Against the wall are trained apple trees, planted by George VI and Queen Elizabeth when they first came to Birkhall as Duke and Duchess of York. Knotted and gnarled, silvery green from the lichen that clothes them, and shaped in espalier fashion, they are picturesque but not fruitful, their curious beauty kept for sentiment and association with past happiness, rather than for usefulness.

Nigella damascena, love–in–the–mist, which is planted among roses in the border under the terrace, has been a justly popular annual for centuries. *Nigella* and *Hyacinthus* from Nicolas Robert, *Diverses Fleurs*, Paris, 1660.

Here's to thee, old apple tree;
Hence thou mayst bud, and whence thou mayst blow,
And whence thou mayst apples bear enow!

(Wassailing song – anonymous)

The broad borders under the terrace wall are planted with blocks of colour and divided by three sets of symmetrically placed descending steps made of wood. Here are dahlias (mostly single varieties), and the floribunda roses 'Lilli Marlene', with scarlet flowers and abundant shining foliage touched with bronze, and 'Anne Cocker', its flowers in bunches of light vermilion. The spaces between the permanent plants are filled by annuals: *Lavatera trimestris* is used, marigolds (*Calendula officinalis*), and love–in–the–mist (*Nigella damascena*),

Looking down on the garden from the terrace in the fullness of August.

one of the loveliest of annual flowers. Gerard tells us it 'is both fair and pleasant', and he illustrates it in his herbal exactly as we see it today; it was grown in English gardens by the Elizabethans, and every cottager had it in his garden by the sixteenth century. Its flowers of misty blue peep from a frill of bright green fine-cut foliage, and it will sow itself, coming up year after year and lasting well into the winter.

In the spring narcissus and daffodils are planted in front of the hybrid teas, and in other beds and borders too, providing a scented show for Queen Elizabeth's visit early in the year.

It is the time of wind and sun
Morning day, and the winter done
Morning life, and the spring begun.

ALICE MEYNELL

Below these borders, on the terrace, there is a steep grass bank, once planted with vegetables, flowers and strawberries but put down to grass by the Queen Mother and now a rich green. A long flight of steps descends the bank to the lower garden, and on either side of these steps, cut out of the turf, is Queen Elizabeth's monogram, ER, planted with French marigolds (*Tagetes patula*), white alyssum (*Alyssum maritima*) and dark blue *Lobelia erinus* 'Crystal Palace'. 'One will do for the Queen and the other for me,' said the Queen Mother. This type of conceit was much used by gardeners in the past, especially in Tudor and Elizabethan times, an example being Henry VIII's monogram in the gardens at Hampton Court.

Mr Kerr has cut the initials ER out of the turf on either side of the steps leading to the terrace, and fills them with annuals. 'One will do for the Queen and the other for me!' says the Queen Mother.

Above: The Italian garden at Glamis Castle, the home of the Bowes Lyon family and an acknowledged influence on Queen Elizabeth's own gardening style.
Opposite: At Crathes Castle, only a few miles from Birkhall, a clipped Portuguese laurel provides a focus for borders of soft coloured old-fashioned plants.

The gravel path which leads from the foot of these steps encircles a fat topiaried yew – a cottage loaf of a yew – with comfortable round bottom and a little loaf on top, and continues to the bottom of the garden ending at the approach to the river, where there are pillars of clipped yew on either side of the path. It is striking here, as we look at these pieces of topiary, how the imagination is stimulated by the variations in mass and outline. Simple as they are, they pull the garden together, marking with perpendicular and solid lines the long walk and emphasizing the salient point of the enclosure. Nothing can give a finer character to a garden than topiary, and these pieces, together with the low clipped hedges of white heath and the boundary hedge of beech, provide a foil for the brilliant colours of the flowers and bring a measure of increased beauty and richness to the whole garden site.

With our back to the river we move up the path which mounts the slope on the left-hand side of the 'bell'. Here there are broad beds on our left, and a narrow border edging the vegetable ground on our right hand is filled with night-scented stock (*Matthiola bicornis*). This is a frail and delicate-looking plant but is perfectly hardy; its flowers are quite undistinguished, but as the twilight falls and darkness overtakes the garden, they exhale a heavenly scent.

Godetias, the colour of ripe apricots, viewed Her Majesty tells me with especial affection by herself, are planted in a broad band with asters 'King Edward' and with *Cosmos bipinnatus*, its feathery foliage and flowers of white and pale and deep pink in the background. Then come quantities of antirrhinums, an intermediate variety in mixed colours, and in the broad beds, besides various herbaceous plants, there is a huge patch of the Shasta daisy (*Chrysanthemum maximum*). A bed of roses is planted with the coppery-pink hybrid tea called 'Remember Me', given to Queen Elizabeth by the National Trust in 1984, and a group of the floribunda 'Europeana', its dark crimson flowers, with tough petals that stand up strongly against the weather, showing well against the coppery-green foliage. These plantings form a picture which reminds one of Matthew Arnold's description of a garden in his poem 'Thesis'.

> *Soon will we have gold-dusted snapdragon,*
> *Sweet William with his homely cottage smell,*
> *And stocks in fragrant blow;*
> *Roses that down the alleys shine afar,*
> *And open, jasmine-muffled lattices*
> *And groups under the dreaming garden trees,*
> *And the full moon, and the white, Evening Star.*

From here the path winds steeply, so steeply that it has to turn into little plank-faced steps which rise in a rough 'S' shape to a heather-thatched summerhouse at their summit. 'In every garden there must be, wherever there may be seclusion, quiet retreats for rest and retirement for contemplation.' So wrote Reynolds Hole, Dean of Rochester, the great rosarian. I am told by the retired gardeners that it was here, in this small summerhouse, that the King used sometimes to sit after his illness; spread below is a panorama of the garden and, beyond its boundaries, a view over the river to the hills, vague with misty blues.

Before climbing the steps we turn left through a small wicket gate set in the hedge, and find ourselves on a narrow path leading into the woodland. On our right hand there is a grass bank thick with *Vinca minor*, which is known as 'Periwinkle Brae' – thousands of celandines open their shiny-gold petals to the

---

Opposite: Queen Elizabeth spends a lot of time in her garden, exercising her dogs on its slopes and taking a close interest in the plants and flowers. The rockery below the summerhouse is a special love, and Her Majesty likes to tend it personally.

sun, and the ancient double daffodil rises through the stiff 'hair-hung' leaves of a carex. The trees are beech and yew with wild cherry, its blossom, when it comes, hanging like white clouds about the woodland. 'Loveliest of trees the cherry now, Is hung with bloom along the bough,' sang Housman, and who can argue with his choice; the milky-white blossom is hung against the faint blue sky of this kindly day of spring, the almost black stems of the trees emphasizing their purity.

The path we are on ends in a bridge, with hazel boughs trained along its handrail, and this leads us on to an island in the river, its waters swirling and dashing fiercely around it. The Muick has twice been flooded in the last sixteen years, and a great deal of snowberry is planted to prevent erosion from the flooding. The fresh young leaves of conifers, larch and birch cast a sweet but indefinable scent on the air in spring, and beneath them is a carpet of the wild wood anemone, the nodding flowers of milky white mingling with the lopping fronds of ferns and bracken and the spears of carex leaves. The branches of the trees encompass a small Gothic sun house, put here in 1910 and now gently mouldering in their shade. Here and there are bushes of broom (*Spartium scoparium*) and there is a blanket of *Gaultheria procumbens* (creeping wintergreen); the insignificant flowers of this evergreen turn into clusters of pinkish-crimson berries and make a lush ground covering. One of the most wonderful aspects of the garden at Birkhall is the autumnal colour of the woodlands and this wild garden, where the butter yellow of the larches, the crimson foliage of the geans and the glistening leaves of the birches, guinea-gold in the mild, low-travelling sun of autumn days, have an arresting beauty.

We must now leave the island and return to the garden proper, regaining the narrow, stepped path and turning right towards the bow-fronted wing of the house. Here on our left is a rock garden, made fourteen years ago, where Queen Elizabeth quite often likes to work herself, planting small things she has found in the countryside around Birkhall, or weeding among the alpine plants that grow in the pockets of earth and spread over the stone. *Daphne retusa* is here, its wonderfully scented flowers appearing at the time of Her Majesty's spring visit, with miniature narcissus, gentians and polyanthus, sedums and saxifrages, and *Primula* 'Wanda', a very ancient primrose known in the seventeenth century, with vivid magenta flowers. Crocus and *Muscari armeniacum* (the grape hyacinth) grow here too; the latter's name comes from *moschos*, musk, which refers to the scent of the variety *M. moschatum*, and its brilliant blue colouring is set off well by the other small flowering plants around it. Later in the year *Santolina incana*, now a silvery grey hump, will produce butter-yellow flowers, and a shrubby potentilla will bloom in primrose colours. Ferns tuck themselves in crevices of the rock, and a celmisia (probably *lyalli*) with spear-shaped leaves, looking as if made of metal, has a white, golden-centred daisy flower. *Bergenia*

Viola lutea grandiflora

Viola lutea grandiflora, from Nicolas Robert's *Diverses Fleurs*, 1660. Queen Elizabeth has planted her beloved pansies in the rockery and the borders by the house.

---

purpurascens grows here too, a native of the Himalayas and China with rosy-purple flowers and the strange English name of 'pig squeak', and some little heartsease pansies (*Viola tricolor*), which were much loved by the Elizabethans and called by many names – 'Johnny-jump-ups' and 'Pinkeney John' among them, though the one that is the most charming is 'Love-in-idleness', conjuring up in a fanciful imagination lovers in a happy pensive mood. *Pulsatilla vulgaris* is another ancient and romantic flower found here – native to the English downs, it is said to grow in the wild only where Saxon blood has been spilt. Flowering at Eastertide, its English name is Easter-flower or Pasque-flower; its buds look like silky mice, and its dull-lilac flowers open among furry, silvery sepals.

There is another small rock garden further along the terrace, at its northern end, from where we can look down on a fine lime tree at the foot of the slope. It has a *Daphne collina* growing against one of the rocks, lily-of-the-valley and golden marjoram provide sweetness and grace, while *Alyssum saxatile* is a heap of clotted gold in spring. Later a shrubby potentilla without a name produces its single white flowers, and in the autumn that covetable lime-hater, *Gentiana sino-ornata*, so hard to grow well outside Scotland, flourishes, its trumpets of dazzling blue appearing finger high above a mat of clear green foliage.

We turn towards the house now, and see the plantings around its white walls. These have to be repainted every five years so it is not easy to deal with climbing plants; consequently there are not many, but there is one beautiful one, the rose 'New Dawn', an especial favourite of Queen Elizabeth, who even has it growing in large pots in the house at Royal Lodge. It has shiny apple green foliage and its sugar-pink flowers smell like a bowl of ripe fruit. It came from the United States in 1930, and is a sport of 'Dr W. Van Fleet', who is as beautiful as his child but only flowers once; his offspring, after an abundance of blossom at midsummer, flowers again, though not so generously.

The silvery-pink flowers of 'New Dawn' are in agreeable harmony with the plantings in the borders round the house, for here summer flowers, following the spring bedding of hyacinths, tulips and *Muscari armeniacum*, with an edging of old-fashioned polyanthus, are packed in with not an inch to spare. Palest pink begonias, East Lothian stocks, *Salvia horminum* and pansies are planted throughout. The silver deeply cut leaves of *Cineraria maritima* are an ideal foil for the washed tints of the flowers – the greenish-white, purple and pink of the salvia, the same colours in the stocks, and a marvellous pansy with white-edged purple velvet flowers called 'Rippling Waters'. A clump of hollyhocks, some with flowers of palest pink, others of darkest wine or, as described by Parkinson, 'dark red like black blood', lean against the wall of the house. The gently blended colours and diverse shapes are a most satisfying and harmonious sight, while a delicious wholesome and vigorous scent pervades the air and must waft through open windows on late summer evenings. There are French windows from the drawing-room in the new wing, which open on to a path that runs alongside the wall borders. From here there is a view away to the village of Ballater and the hills beyond, partially screened by a wrought-iron gate set in a tall and massive hedge of × *Cupressocyparis leylandii* that acts as an essential windbreak and helps to create a sheltered area by the house. The gate, which is intricately fashioned with vines and other fruits, was a first prizewinner at the Royal Highland Show some thirty years ago.

The climbing rose 'New Dawn' is a special favourite of Queen Elizabeth, who even has it growing in large pots in the house at Royal Lodge.

The Queen Mother at the Braemar Games. The Royal Family do much in support of the Highland community when they are in Scotland.

From the door in the old part of the house on to this same path there is a flight of steps, the handrail of wrought iron, elegantly shaped and entwined with a honeysuckle (*Lonicera belgica*) which was given to the Queen Mother as an eightieth birthday present by the Crathie Women's Guild; its scent too reaches into the house through open windows on balmy summer evenings, but is sweeter still in the early morning. It is a British native and bears one of the oldest flower names, known in the early part of the eighth century.

> The Honeysuckle that groweth wild on every hedge, although it be very sweete, yet doe I not bring it into my garden, but let it rest in his owne place, to serve their senses that travel by it, or have no garden . . .

wrote Parkinson in *Paradisus Terrestris* (1629). We see it peeping from the hedges in the afternoon of the year, and waving its flowers from the heart of blackberry bushes on the downs. Its divine scent is inextricably bound in our minds with fields of golden grain and the abundance of harvest.

Just beyond the bowed end of the new wing, and built at the same time, is a place arranged for sitting out – the bank that rises up beyond the house at this point being cut away and lined and floored with stone from the old city tram lines of Aberdeen – but this has not been altogether a success as it is too sheltered from the sun.

On the western side of the house a rose garden has been arranged. Here the ground rises in gentle undulations behind the topmost summerhouse. The grass is planted with many late narcissi, to please the Queen Mother with their scent in May. There used to be a little orchard at the summit of the bank, but the old trees produced no fruit and their place has been taken by a wild cherry and a beautiful golden-leaved tree, rare and interesting; it is a Mediterranean oak, *Quercus alnifolia*, the 'golden oak' of Cyprus. Doubtfully hardy and very slow-growing, it seems to have settled in well at Birkhall. Nearby a round bed has been cut out in the grass and filled with floribunda roses – they are varieties we have seen elsewhere in the garden, 'Honeymoon', 'Marlena' and 'Coronation', a rose lower in height and paler in colour. This slope rises behind the rock garden and here there is another circular bed, this time planted with the rose 'Crathes Castle', given to the Queen Mother on her eightieth birthday by the National Trust who now own the garden there. There is a long border of yellow roses – the modern shrub rose 'Chinatown', 5 feet tall, its deep yellow flowers wonderfully scented.

Behind this is an un-named rambling rose, trained on wires, and sprinkled in the grass about it are the sky-blue flowers of harebells. A little beyond and providing shelter from the western winds are two noble copper beeches, an ancient larch tree, a Douglas fir or two, a fine old yew and a massive old *Sequoia sempervirens*, the tree that lives longer and grows taller than any other – when one was felled it was discovered to be 2,200 years old, and another measured 360 feet in height. It has a brown-red bark that is soft and spongy when you punch it.

Descending again to the house, we see tucked into a west-facing corner a square filled with the delightful 'Connemara Heath' (*Daboecia cantabrica bicolor*), with white, pink and even some striped flowers, borne in racemes from June to November. *Cotoneaster horizontalis*, a mass of tiny white flowers in summer and scarlet berries in autumn, fans out its stiff branches against the wall not far from a buddleia, whose grey velvety leaves and palest mauve flowers show well against the white-washed house.

Skilful planning as well as devoted work must be behind the creation of a garden which is so full of interest when the Queen Mother comes to stay; she spends many happy hours wandering around it, admiring the beauty and vigour of her plants and tending her favourite alpines. At much-loved Birkhall, full of happy memories for Her Majesty, and a place little changed since she was here as Duchess of York, she is able to enjoy in peace and seclusion the pleasures of her charming garden.

Epilogue

The four gardens of Queen Elizabeth The Queen Mother which I have been visiting, so diverse in geographical position, layout and aspect, seem linked together into a harmonious whole by four distinct strands. The first of these strands is 'attention', the care with which all Her Majesty's gardens are tended; the second 'love'; the third 'knowledge', the experience which teaches a gardener the art of plant association and of adapting to a particular climate; and the fourth 'personal taste'. The four gardens are indeed different in many ways, but these strands, weaving through each garden, create a similarity of atmosphere, feeling and manner brought to them by the taste, love, attention and knowledge of their owner.

In medieval times the pleasure garden was made among fruit trees, vegetables and herbs. Many grand gardens later had separate sections for flowers, vegetable growing and fruit orchards, but in some places the old tradition lingered with charming effect, as in the gardens of Queen Elizabeth, where vegetables, fruit and flowers mingle happily.

Gardening is the most ephemeral of arts – usually, and ideally, the creation of one mind, character and personality. The creator is devoted to achieving in reality a vision of the ideal, a vision of a garden perfectly situated, and full of ideas conceived and realized with an artistry both aesthetically pleasing and able at the same time to please all the senses. The garden will express in every way the skills of its creator. After studying these four gardens of Her Majesty I feel I can say as did John Gerard in the year 1597 'that the excellent art of . . . gardening hath been a study for the wisest, an exercise for the robust, a pastime for the best'.

Opposite: Queen Elizabeth The Queen Mother admires *Campanula persicifolia* 'Loddon Anna' at Royal Lodge. Throughout the year Her Majesty finds peace and contentment in her four gardens.

Acknowledgements

I owe many debts of gratitude to all the people who have helped in the creation of this book and I would like to thank them.

Firstly, it could not have been undertaken without the gracious permission of Her Majesty Queen Elizabeth The Queen Mother. I am deeply honoured and grateful that she should have granted it and should have spared me so much of her precious time, as well as for her help, encouragement and interest which made my visits to the gardens such a joy and delight.

I am grateful, too, to the Members of Her Majesty's Household and Estate Offices, and particularly to Sir Martin Gilliat G.C.V.O. and Sir Alastair Aird K.C.V.O who were unfailingly helpful and patient over endless inquiries and requests; to John Bond (Director of the Savill and Valley Gardens and of the gardens at Royal Lodge) who helped in several ways, not least in putting right my identification of certain plants, and to Her Majesty's gardeners, Paddy Bennett at Royal Lodge, Terri-Janina Bijowska and Bennie White at Clarence House, Sandy Webster at the Castle of Mey and James Kerr at Birkhall.

For their help with research I should like to thank Robin Harcourt-Williams, our Librarian at Hatfield House, Theresa-Mary Morton at the Royal Library, Windsor, and the staff at the Royal Horticultural Society's Lindley Library and at the Tradescant Trust. I have been very lucky to have Derry Moore's superb photographs alongside my text, and at times his charming company, and am also grateful to Alice Munro-Faure for unearthing so many interesting supplementary photographs and to Jennifer Johnson and Marjorie Selby for so efficiently deciphering my tangled scribbles and typing them beautifully.

To Celia Van Oss my debt is enormous. For her patient help, wise advice and delightful companionship on our many expeditions to the gardens in fair weather and foul, I shall always be grateful. I want to thank Eleo Gordon too, for her endless good humour, patience and help.

Finally, I would like to thank my husband for good-humouredly putting up with my marriage to a book for so many months.

The following books proved very useful: *Trees and Shrubs Hardy in the British Isles*, W. J. Bean (8th ed); *House of Gordon*, J. M. Bulloch (1903); *The History of the King's Works*, ed. H. M. Colvin (1976); *Sylva*, John Evelyn (1664); *The Origins of Garden Plants*, John Fisher (1982); *The Herball or General History of Plants*, John Gerard (1633); *A Modern Herbal*, Mrs M. Greive (1931); *Queen Adelaide*, Mary Hopkirk (1946); *Paradisi In Sole Paradisus Terrestris*, John Parkinson (1629); *The Gardens in the Royal Park at Windsor*, Lanning Roper (1959); *The Royal Gardeners: King George and His Queen*, W. Shewell-Cooper (1952); and *The Renaissance Garden in England*, Roy Strong (1979).

All the photographs, except those listed below, are © Derry Moore. The drawings on pages 17, 55, 105 and 149 are by Phillida Gili.

Grateful acknowledgement is made to the following for permission to reproduce illustrations in the text:

Royal Horticultural Society (photographs Eileen Tweedy) endpapers, 38, 69, 97 *(left)*, 123, 131, 142, 143, 173, 175, 183; Lord Chamberlain's Office, © Her Majesty The Queen 8, 57; Her Majesty Queen Elizabeth The Queen Mother 9, 15, 118; Syndication International 10, 145; Camera Press London 11; BBC Hulton Picture Library 12, 159; Harry Smith Horticultural Photographic Collection 13, 27, 30, 32, 33, 47, 49, 77 *(left)*, 81, 89, 90, 95, 98 *(right)*, 101, 102, 126, 128, 133, 138, 163, 170, 179, 185; Norman Parkinson (Camera Press London) 14; Windsor Castle, Royal Library © Her Majesty The Queen 18, 23, 152; Royal Commission on the Historical Monuments of England (D. McCarthy) 21; The Marchioness of Salisbury 24, 83, 85, 92, 154; Aerofilms 26; Studio Lisa (Camera Press London) 28; Cecil Beaton (Camera Press London) 34; Celia Van Oss 52, 93; Richard Slade (Camera Press London) 60; City of Westminster Libraries Archives and Local Studies Section 58, 66, 70, 71; National Portrait Gallery London 61; A–Z Collection 77 *(right)*, 98 *(left)*, 122, 165; Bennie White 87; The Trustees of the Victoria and Albert Museum 97 *(right)*; Sotheby's 106 *(left)*, 108, 139, 153, 157, 158, 160; Royal Commission on Ancient Monuments, Scotland 106 *(right)*; Rex Features 151, 186; Strathmore Estate 178.

Index

Rosa Prouincialis Dod.   *R. cùm priое.*